Butterfly of Hope
Finding My Wings

JoAnn Santore Dickson

D1569928

Contents

Dedicated to...
I want to dedicate this book to Ilchi Lee, my Spiritual Guide and teacher who taught me how to love and heal myself and Randy, my husband and soul mate, who stood by my side through most of it all!

Disclaimer for Body & Brain Practitioner Memoir

This book is intended to give the reader a glimpse into my personal, spiritual journey. Its contents consist of opinions, reflections, and recollections that are solely my own (JoAnn Dickson) and do not necessarily represent the views, statements, or opinions of individuals and organizations which I mention. I may make references to an individual or organizations, or their artwork, music, books, programs, or other materials because I consider them a part of my journey, but this does not constitute an endorsement by them.

A Letter to the Reader

Dear Reader,

Thank you for opening this book about my life. I hope you find inspiration, hope and humor in these pages.

Through writing this book I have learned a lot about my past and had the ability to sort through things from a different perspective. I can let go of the guilt and shame now, realizing how much I grew from the experiences I had.

I love and accept myself unconditionally now and I hope you can do the same for yourself. Life is a journey and always remember "Obstacles are an opportunity for your growth!"

Wishing you Health, Happiness & Peace!

JoAnn

Contact me at Norridge@BodynBrain.com or 708-716-3106 with any questions or if you'd like to set up a Coaching Call to talk about how I can help you!

Please leave a review on Amazon and let me know what you identified with in my book, or what you learned. Thank you!

PS Please be aware there is sexually explicit content in this book and not all of it is consensual.

Life Changes in a Moment

You do not just wake up and become the butterfly. Growth is a process.

Once the van stopped spinning, we were facing the opposite direction against the curb on the four-lane road. The smell of burnt rubber filled the car.

It was September 1996. I was headed home from my son Nicholas's 10th birthday party at Lazer Zone. In my minivan, I had my son, five of his friends, and my daughter, Teresa, who was six years old.

The van was bouncing with excitement as the boys shared their stories about the fun they'd had shooting each other at the party. "I only got shot twice," one of the boys gloated, "and I found the best hiding spot."

"I wish we could have stayed longer. It was awesome!" Nicholas said.

I just turned on to Golf Road, heading west at 45 miles per hour. I asked Teresa, "Did you have fun, honey?"

"Yes, it was cool running around shooting at everyone. Can I have my birthday party there too?"

"Wouldn't you rather do something girl-"

Suddenly there was a jolt and a loud crash from the back of the van, and we started spinning around like a top. Coins from my dashboard flew around, and excitement changed to fear.

"Is everyone okay?" I asked.

Small voices from the back seats answered, "I think so."

"I'm scared," one of them said.

One boy hit his head on the side of the car, and another felt the force of the seatbelt digging into his chest, everyone was shaken but seemed okay.

My husband, Randy, was in his car ahead of us with our 12-year-old son, Alex, and a couple of his friends. They heard the crashing of the cars and saw our van spinning around in the rear-view mirror and back window.

"My god. Is everyone ok?" My husband asked as the side door of the van opened.

"I think so. What the hell happened?" I spurted out.

"It looks like that small red chevy must have rammed into the back of the van. I think it's an older woman in the driver's seat."

The red chevy was in the middle of the road so the traffic was starting to slow down, checking things out and going around the scene of the accident.

"I can't believe this happened," I said. "I'm so glad nobody is hurt, and they were all buckled in. Is she blind? How could she not see our van?"

Sounds of sirens and flashing lights appeared in the distance and grew closer and louder. I'm not sure who called the police, but they arrived shortly after the accident.

The sun was going down, and the sky was getting darker. Gloomy silence had shattered all the excitement in our van.

"Is everyone all right?" The police arrived, flashlights moving from face to face and shining into the eyes of the frightened young boys.

"It looks like she hit the back of the van in just the right spot to make it spin," Randy spoke in amazement.

"Is she drunk? What the hell happened? I have a car full of kids. She shouldn't be driving if she can't see a van," I said.

The policeman spoke, "It's an older woman. She appears a little confused. I don't think she's hurt. But we're gonna take her in to have her checked."

"Something must be wrong with her. I'm responsible for all these kids. Someone could have really been hurt."

I took a few breaths to calm myself, realizing at that moment what could have happened. Gratitude began to fill my heart now. Tears welled up in my eyes. "I can't believe this happened."

"Can we go home now? I have to get everyone home. We should call their parents and let them know what's going on since we're late, so they don't worry."

Randy helped with the police report, since he was a witness. We received our copy of the papers, and now everyone shaken to silence, we were on our way.

Once all the kids were safe with their parents, I felt relieved. It could have been so much worse. I didn't want to think about the possibilities of how it could have turned out.

Randy and I talked about how fortunate we were that nobody was hurt as we lay in bed that night. Before I knew it, he was breathing slow and steady, fast asleep. I was still awake thinking about how fragile life was and how it could have changed in an instant.

In my journal a couple days after the accident, I wrote:

My kids and Randy are my life. I don't know what I'd do if something happened to any of them. I don't want to think about what could have been. I'm grateful everyone is okay. We are blessed. Thank you, God.

I never thought much about how precious each moment was until then. My minivan was a taxi service taking the kids to their friends' houses, school, and wherever they needed to go. I was the cook, maid, and the one who made sure they had clothes, supplies and projects done so they could thrive in school and social activities.

I also focused on updating the house and buying new décor for our home. These things seemed so trivial now. In one split second, our lives could have changed dramatically. That night, possibilities of horrifying outcomes which could have taken place went through my head. Parents had entrusted me with the safety of their children. Anyone of us could have been hurt, crippled, or even killed.

I found out that the older woman who hit us was coming home from the hospital after visiting a sick friend that night. Although she was pretty shaken up by the accident, she was unharmed.

What I didn't realize at the time was that sometimes physical symptoms can be invisible at first and might take days or even weeks before they begin to surface.

After the Accident

♥

I worked at a dental supply manufacturing facility near our house. The parking lot was in the back of the factory, and I had to walk to the front of the building to go into the lobby and get to my desk in the office. The walk was a couple of blocks long and took some time before I could get to my desk.

In the office, there were sets of cubicles for each department. I was in the Human Resource Department. I oversaw setting up and making any changes to employees' benefits. My days were spent mostly on the computer, sometimes getting up to talk to payroll or my boss. The filing cabinets were around the corner from my desk, near my boss's.

My boss was a kindhearted woman. She was always having to put out fires relating to the members insurance and benefits. She took her responsibilities seriously. When she wasn't busy, we chatted about our families.

She had one young adult son, and he was her world. We discussed his relationships and how his life was going.

I always had something going with my three kids. "How are your kids these days? Any news about Teresa and those girls that are being mean to her at school?" she would ask me.

"Randy brings her home for lunch most of the time, so she doesn't have to deal with all of it. I can't believe how cruel kids can be. It breaks my heart. I encourage her to hang out with the girls she's comfortable with and ignore the others. I wish they would just leave her alone."

The payroll woman and I worked closely together also. We both had young families and talked when there was time. She had a son who was handicapped, and she always worried about him.

Once payroll was completed, we had time to chat. "How's your son doing in school?" I would ask.

"He has his days. Sometimes he gets frustrated that he can't do the things the others can, and I feel bad for him. This is just part of life for him. He's such a sweet boy and loves his brother and sister so much. He never complains, he just goes along and smiles and laughs whenever he is around them," she would share.

"I wish kids could be more compassionate," I would answer. "It sounds like he's got a great spirit and attitude."

I sat at the computer most of the time entering benefit information and any changes that were required for payroll. Employees would come to me with questions or adjustments, and I would fill out the proper paperwork and process the changes. I also had to make copies of everything for our files.

The bathroom and cafeteria were all the way on the other side of the office. It was a nice break to get up and stretch my legs and chat with people on the way after working on the computer so much.

Two weeks after the accident, I got up from my desk heading to the bathroom. My head began to pull to my right side and toward my shoulder. The muscles in my neck began to spasm, and I couldn't control my posture.

"Are you okay?" one of my coworkers asked as he saw me struggling to hold my head straight.

"I don't know. My neck feels tight, and I can't hold my head straight. I'm not sure what's going on."

"Ok, hope you feel better," he wasn't sure what to say.

I tried to collect myself by pushing my head upright with my hand, which didn't make much of a difference, as I got myself to the bathroom. I felt like an odd spectacle and wanted to go sit down and hide. I went back to my desk and didn't know what to do. When I sat down the spasms lessened, but I didn't feel normal. I wanted to go home now.

"I'm not feeling well and need to go home and lay down," I told my boss. I didn't want to talk about what I was experiencing. I just wanted to go home to rest, hoping it would pass.

"Did you finish entering the changes for payroll?" she asked. She was so involved in her own work she didn't notice the pain I was in.

"I have a few more things to enter. I'll get it done before I leave."

"Ok, take care." She put her nose back to her papers; it wasn't a good time to talk. Days before payroll were the busiest.

I stumbled out the door and to my car, hoping nobody would notice me holding my neck. Driving home while trying to hold my neck up with my hand, I felt desperate. Luckily the kids had other plans after school, and I didn't have to pick them up.

Randy came home and found me lying in bed instead of cooking dinner.

He was surprised, "Honey, are you okay? Aren't you feeling well?"

"I'm not sure what's going on," I said in a scared voice. "My neck is tight, and its moving on its own. I can't hold it straight." I started to sob.

"Maybe you need to go to the doctor. Can I do something for you? Are you hungry?"

"I'm not hungry. I'm gonna just rest. Maybe you should just order something for you and the kids. Sorry I didn't cook. I'm scared. This feels so strange."

While I was laying down, my muscles could rest, so everything seemed better. I slept through the night hoping to forget about what happened that day.

As I got up from bed the next day, my distorted posture returned. My neck muscles could not support my head, but I couldn't lay in bed all day. I had to get the kids ready for school and myself ready for work. Randy had to get to work before me so he couldn't help as much as he wanted to.

"Are you okay? Do you want me to go in late or stay home to help you?" he asked.

"No, I'll be okay. You have to get to work. I'll manage. If I don't feel well, I'll come home early," I responded automatically.

I started moving about, getting ready, supporting my head with my hand to avoid the pain and awkwardness of the spasms. I had three young kids that depended on me to get them to school, so I did what I needed to do. I had to make lunches, check homework, and get everyone out the door on time. Driving was another challenge, holding one hand on the steering wheel and the other on my neck to push my head toward my center while also pushing back into the seat for support.

Next, I had to get to work. I carried my lunch bag with one hand and my head in the other. If I had a bottle of water or anything extra, I wouldn't have had enough hands. My unsupported head would have stayed tilted and painful for the long walk. I couldn't wait to sit in my chair and hide from any questions. All I wanted was to get to my desk and be alone. When I was sitting, I could do my work and manage my crooked neck. I dreaded the thought of anyone coming to see me. I might have to answer questions about why my neck was crooked now.

As the days went on, the spasms started to get more painful, and the involuntary movements of my head got worse. People started to ask if I was okay, and I answered briefly, "yes," trying to avoid the subject and just get through the day and go home.

At home, I would go to bed early to avoid more pain being upright any longer than I needed to. I was in survival mode.

Being raised Christian Science, I avoided going to the doctor unless it was totally necessary, like a broken limb or inability to breathe or excruciating pain.

Mom was raised as a Christian Scientist and practiced by reading her *Bible* and *Key to the Scriptures* by Mary Baker Eddy books daily. My sister and I went to Sunday School while she attended church most Sundays. Dad would drop us off and pick us up, but he never stayed. He would go home and wash the car or cut the grass or do something around the house.

The basis of the Christian Science religion is believing that we are spiritual beings, the reflection of Christ, a perfect being. The body is denied, since Christ has no body, he is spiritual. Any kind of issue with the body is recognized as erroneous thinking. This is the way I understood it.

As a young girl I studied these beliefs regularly using the *Bible* and *Key to the Scriptures* like my mom. One time I felt sick and didn't want to miss school the next day, so I studied and prayed all night. The next day, I woke up and was miraculously better. I practiced mind over matter, and it worked.

Maybe the thought still existed in my subconscious that I could heal myself. At this point I wasn't practicing Christian Science beliefs, but I believed in a higher power and that natural healing was a possibility for certain conditions.

Life as a Caterpillar

♥

As children, we are caterpillars living under the influence of others' emotions and ego.

T he earliest memories of my life I remember being carefree and loving. As I grew, I realized things weren't always as I thought they should be. People were not kind to each other, judging and criticizing one another. Also, priorities weren't always in the right order. In my family, it was clear that materials were more important than children and their feelings. I awakened to the sad state of humanity as a small child.

I was the youngest of four children. My oldest brother David was thirteen years old when I was born; Rick was twelve; and April was just over three years old. My parents had two sets of kids a decade apart. My sister and I grew up together. I felt alone most of the time, but then maybe it was my perception.

I loved to spend time outside when the weather was pleasant.

"Mom, can I have a picnic outside today for lunch?" I would ask.

"I guess so. Go get the blanket from downstairs, and I'll make your rye toast with butter." Mom said yes!

Having picnics outside was my favorite thing to do. Laying in the cool grass looking up at the sky and hearing the bird songs always comforted me.

Inside the house wasn't always a happy place.

"Why is Dad so crabby when he comes home from work?"

"He works hard, and he doesn't want to be bothered. Just behave yourself, and he'll be happy."

"Nadine's parents play games with them at night. Can we try that?"

"Just watch TV and relax. We want to watch our shows."

"Dad's going to paint the back room this weekend, so you'll need to stay out of the way."

"Okay."

My parents gave me a roof over my head, clothes to wear, food, and all those necessary things that I needed to survive. Being the fourth child and second daughter in my family, I believe they did the best they could with what they knew and was possible.

Being the youngest in my family, and of all the cousins, I was always too young to be included in activities and conversations. Eventually, I became self-conscious and lonely. The older cousins were close in age. They played softball and Monkey in the Middle. I had to be the monkey if I wanted to play. My cousins next door had a pool, and the water was above my head. I couldn't swim. I was left alone and called a cry baby many times.

I felt like I always had to push my way into conversations.

At the dinner table, I wanted to talk about my day.

"Debbie got a cute outfit for her Barbie, and she said they got it at Golf Mill. Can we go look this weekend?"

My parents and sister were usually watching the news or Andy Griffith on the Zenith TV which was mounted on the wall at the end of the table

"Shh, I want to hear the tv. You always talk when I want to hear something." Dad would say.

This hurt my feelings as a young child. Raising my kids, I never allowed a tv in our kitchen. I wanted to hear everything about my kid's thoughts and experiences.

"This weekend Dad will be working in the back room. Play with what you have. There are some old clothes in the closet. Make something yourself."

"Okay, I'll see what's in there."

"Make sure you put the clothes back in the bag when you're done."

Most of the time, it felt like my opinion or thoughts didn't matter. I remember a time when I tried to add to a conversation between my brother and sister hoping to fit in. They were talking about friends not having a ride to the mall. "Maybe they could come with us," I said.

"JoAnn, you don't know what you're talking about. You're just stupid. Go play with your dolls."

I will never forget when my big brother said this to me. Somehow, I hoped I could add to their conversation this time, speaking honestly. After that, I spent a lot of time in my room alone.

Mom kept a neat and tidy house and always had dinner on the table when Dad would arrive home after work. She fulfilled her duties as homemaker and mom. She never got a driver's license or worked outside the home after starting her family. I was sad for her staying in the house most of the time, cleaning, and cooking for everyone, but she seemed content with her life.

Dad worked hard as a mechanic and was always upgrading the house in some way in his spare time and had a new car every 2 years or so. These were the priorities in his life. Having a nice house and a new car was success in his mind.

Sometimes, I would accidentally spill my pop on the dinner table. My father would tsk in disbelief, face growing red with anger, head nodding in disgust. Then he would burst into a rage, "What's the matter with this kid? Look at the mess. It's getting all over the floor. Get the towel. JoAnn, go to your room now."

Shrinking with my tail between my legs, I would do as I was told.

I never understood why my mom didn't protect me. Why did she allow him to be so mean to me? Were these really my parents? They didn't act like they loved me. All they cared about was their house and furniture.

Dad always watched me like a hawk when I would try to help by doing dishes or any chores. "Shirl, do you see what she's doing? She's making a big mess. Look at the water dripping on the cabinets," tsking as always after.

"Go and play now. I'll finish up," Mom would tell me.

I loved crafts. For birthdays and Christmas, I asked for any kind of craft kit.

"I want to make some bracelets for my friends. Can we go to Tandy Crafts and get some more beads and elastic? Maybe you could make some too." I asked my mom.

"I have to clean the house and cook dinner before your dad gets home. Find one of your friends to go, and I'll give you a few dollars. Go check my purse to see what I have."

The rotary phone was on the wall in the kitchen. Inserting my finger into the small, numbered circles, I dialed Nadine's number. Stretching the cord to my room across the hall, I closed the door.

"Hello, this is JoAnn. Is Nadine home?" I called my friend.

"Hello."

"Can you play today? Do you want to go get some beads for making jewelry? My mom gave me some money."

"I can't play today. I have to clean my room," she answered.

"Okay, call me when you finish and maybe we can go later."

Sitting on the back porch, I saw Nadine and her sisters walking their dog Sandy, laughing, and having fun. I watched as they went to Kathy's house next door and knocked on her door.

I ran to my room and cried into my pillow. After settling down I opened my journal to write down the hurt I felt.

Why doesn't anyone like me? I feel so alone.

In school I tried to do my best and help the teachers.

"Mrs. McNulty, can I clean the erasers today?"

"Yes, please, and put all those books back on the shelf for me."

My teachers appreciated my efforts, giving me a pat on the back and a thank you. I loved to help and felt valued by them.

I started to make friends at school.

"I want to go to the sock hop tonight with Maria. Can dad give us a ride?"

"Your father is tired. He wants to relax after dinner."

"Okay, I'll ask if Maria's parents can drive again."

Maria was my best friend in grammar school. I spent a lot of time at her house. Her mom was nice, and they weren't so worried about messes and having a neat and tidy house.

We would talk about our feelings.

"I wish I was pretty," I confided in her.

"You are pretty. You have pretty eyes and wavy hair. You're thin," she said, surprised to hear my thoughts.

"Really, I never thought so. Nobody ever told me that. Are you sure?"

"Yes, I bet the boys like you."

Maybe there was some way of feeling good about myself after all.

I was told that happiness came from the inside but never really understood what that meant so I always wanted to spend more time with friends to fill this emptiness in my heart.

Friends spent quality time together with their families, and I always wished mine could be closer like them. My parents were older when I was born, so maybe that was part of the reason that they were tired and didn't have patience or energy for me.

I don't remember my brothers being around growing up, and my sister was always very involved with what my parents were working on around the house, cleaning or updating. I tried to stay out of the way so I wouldn't get into trouble.

My sister and I took piano lessons, and of course being younger I could not play as well, but I did enjoy playing the piano when I was alone and singing and making up songs too.

I started to enjoy my alone time. I kept journals of my feelings and experiences growing up.

Looking back at some of my journal entries as a girl I realized how simple life was.

Today I wore my purple elephant ears and white top. I liked the way I looked. Maria liked it too. I saw Sam looking at me. Maybe he likes me. I'm not sure what I should do to find out. I'll ask Maria what she thinks. Tomorrow I'll wear my black palazzo pants and pink top.

Around 10 years old, I started to get more involved in Sunday School so I could help with younger kids at the church. We would play games with the kids while their parents attended the church service. This was another opportunity that made me feel more valued and included by others.

Freedom and Choices

♥

Mistakes are part of our growth!

When I turned 11, my parents gave me more freedom to go places with friends. I went to the mall with friends and started having sleepovers. I was never given much money for these outings, but it was great to have something to do with my friends.

Maria and I took the Niles Free Bus to Golf Mill. As young girls we wanted jewelry, make up and clothes that we couldn't afford. We came up with the brilliant idea to put earrings, other inexpensive jewelry, and make up in our pockets and waistbands from Woolworths and JC Penney. We thought this idea was genius. Getting what we wanted and not burdening parents for money, we found a solution. Happy to have more of what we wanted; it was never enough.

One Sunday at JC Penney, a man in a suit and tie approached us. "Come with me," he instructed.

We glanced at each other wide-eyed and shaking in our tight fitted jeans and sneakers as we followed. "Empty your pockets onto the table." There were a couple pairs of earrings, a few necklaces, and a bracelet.

"Girls, do you have money to pay for all of this? What are your names and phone numbers? We have to call your parents. You won't be allowed in this store anymore. You could get in a lot of trouble with the police. If we catch you again, we will call the police."

I guess it was a matter of time, but Sunday wasn't a good day to get caught. My mom was at church. My dad would answer the phone when they called.

Oh boy, what did I do now? Maybe I should run away. This wasn't going to be good.

My dad walked through the door, face red with anger, shaking his bald head as he tsked as always about my behavior. "What the hell is the matter with you, JoAnn?" He slapped my face in front of everyone there.

Tails between our legs, Maria and I followed him to the car. The ride was silent and felt like eternity. What would my parents do to me? This was bad.

I'm not sure what I was thinking. I wanted more stuff than I could get money for, so I took it.

When my mom got home from church she asked me, trembling, tears in her eyes, "Why do you do this to me? You're worse than the boys. I don't know what to do with you."

She told me to get rid of everything that was stolen. I felt bad about what I had done. I had let my desires control my actions. Maybe it was just part of that void I felt, trying to fill it with possessions, just like my parents did with updating the house all the time, but I had to steal since I didn't have enough money.

"I don't want you to see or talk to Maria anymore. You need to make some better friends. She's no good."

I did see her at school every day. My parents couldn't enforce this since I rode my bike to school and came home for dinner when I was supposed to.

Maria was my closest friend. Her mom gave her a hug when she got home and said I know you won't do that anymore. She was a nice girl and a good friend who stood by my side. She seemed to have a much more loving family.

She wasn't looking for love, but I was always seeking love and doing what I could do to be liked by boys. Wearing a size three, I flaunted my body in bra-less fitted T-shirts and cheek length cut offs or tight-fitted blue jeans. Boys would ask if they could put their arm around me to get closer, pretending they liked me and cop a feel. The next day, I would say hello to them, thinking we were friends, and they would ignore me.

At Maine East High School, I met a group of friends that hung out regularly at the house of two cute blonde boys who were brothers. Their mom had died, so their dad was raising them on his own. Most of the time he was drunk, and we hung out in the basement. This is where it all happened.

"It's Friday night, who are we gonna get to buy the beer?" Maria would inquire.

"Does anyone have any weed?" I asked.

"I'll get Andy. He'll be around in an hour. Get the money together. John usually has some pretty good pot. I'll give him a call. I hope he's still got some of that 'Hawaiian' that we smoked last week." One of the brothers said.

"Mom, I'm gonna stay at Karen's house tonight," I'd arranged.

"Ok, behave yourself. Watch what you're doing over there," she would answer.

The basement where we hung out would be full of teens, loud music, cigarette and pot smoke, bongs, and beer. There was a small area in the back of the basement divided with dark curtains. A single bed and couch were in the room along with a black light and posters on the wall. If a couple wanted to make out, have sex, or smoke some special weed or hash they didn't want to share, they would use that space.

The only adult member of the household was either out at the bar or passed out upstairs and never said much of anything. This was the place I smoked pot, tried other drugs, and had a few different boyfriends. I had lots of sleepovers at Karen's, for real and not.

The first time I smoked pot, I didn't feel any difference, but after that I was hooked. "I feel great. Ha ha ha. This is so great. Ha ha ha. Why isn't smoking pot legal? Drinking is legal and people get crazy when they're drunk. This is amazing. I feel so relaxed. Isn't this great? Ha ha ha." I spoke in amazement to my friends.

Toking another hit of the joint as Karen passed it to me, she'd say, "Man, yeah, it's great." She was choking and coughing as she exhaled.

"Turn it up. I love this song. Pink Floyd, Wish You Were Here, yeah." I exclaimed. We sang along, swaying side to side in unison, "So, so you think you can tell. Heaven from Hell. Blue skies from pain. Duh, duh, duh, duh, Wish You Were Here." Lifting the arm up on the record player, to replay the song, we listened a few times and sang along, feeling the music deeply in our bodies.

"Let's go get some munchies. I'm starving." I declared. This was my life in high school on Friday and Saturday nights. I tried some heavier drugs a couple times and didn't like the feeling of being out of control, so pot was my drug of choice. Alcohol made me sick most of the time, so I didn't drink much.

Promiscuity was also part of my free and casual lifestyle in the 70s, which I'm not happy to admit. I guess it was part of experimentation as well as looking outside myself for love. I carry a lot of shame regarding my lack of self-respect at that time.

One evening walking home from my friend's house in Park Ridge cutting through the Country Club, a man came up to me and my friend. Since we were on private property, he had us empty our pockets, and I had some pot in mine. We were taken to the office, and our parents were called. My sister and mom came to pick me up this time. My dad was working nights. Phew.

"JoAnn what is wrong with you? Now, you're smoking pot? What am I going to do with you? You're worse than the boys. You're going to drive me to an early grave. How am I going to tell your father about this? I have to tell him."

"Mom, it isn't bad. It's like alcohol. It helps me relax. They should make it legal."

"I don't want to hear about it. Throw it all away. Do you have more somewhere else? Get rid of it."

One Sunday morning, I decided to meet my mom at church after staying over at a friend's house near the church. I didn't mention that the friend was a boy. I was starting to feel guilty about what I was doing and how I was hurting her. "Tears started to flow during the service, and I cried and cried, releasing the guilt and shame I felt. From her purse, she handed me tissues scented with Wrigley's Double mint gum, and we never spoke a word about it. I knew inside I was on the wrong path but wasn't strong enough to change at the time.

As a young child I always had nervous tics and lots of tension in my body. Sometimes I couldn't fall asleep because my body would continually spasm. Being raised Christian Science, I never said anything to anyone and just accepted that this was normal.

In hindsight, I had a weakened or overactive nervous system that was never diagnosed, which is why I had a strong addiction to smoking marijuana growing up.

I managed to graduate high school half of a semester early. I was friendly with the work program teacher, spending time talking to him in his office like many other girls did. Taking this class earned two credits, one for work and one for class. Most of the time, I went out to get high with friends during the class, but I did work after school part time. I was in this class for two years. He made some inappropriate advances one time, and I moved away, then avoided being alone with him after that. I never told the authorities because I was getting what I needed by not having to go to class and not being reported.

I was able to start the next chapter of my life earlier than most since I was able to graduate high school early. I was ready, in many ways, to move forward.

After finishing high school, my life began to change in more positive ways. I began to grow and change into an adult with my new-found responsibilities. I started my first full-time job at a place called Yamazen USA in Morton Grove., IL. I invoiced customers for the parts that were shipped at a Japanese machinery company and was also helping at the reception desk too. I was ready to be responsible for myself and looking forward to my future hopes and dreams.

I suppose my dreams at the time were to find a man to marry and have a family. Beyond that, I really don't remember any other big dreams.

Meeting My Soul Mate

♥

I have loved you for 1,000 years!

Working at Yamazen, I would visit Meg at the reception desk at break time. One afternoon, a tall guy came in. He had curly brown hair and eyes that sparkled and was dressed in a short-sleeved white button up shirt and blue jeans. "I'm here to see Ross. My name is Randy Dickson."

"Ok, I'll let him know you're here. Are you applying for the warehouse position?" Meg inquired.

"Yes," he said.

After Ross came to get him, Meg and I looked at each other. "He's kind of cute. What do you think?" she asked.

"I hope he gets the job. He is cute and seems like a genuine person," I said. I didn't know where this comment came from, but it just came out. I sensed something different about him.

A while later, I was visiting Meg again, and he was finished with his interview. As he skipped out the door, he updated us. "I got the job! See you in a couple days."

Grinning from ear to ear, we chimed, "Great! See you soon!"

I invoiced customers for the machinery and parts that were shipped daily. Randy brought me the paperwork for what was shipped, and if there was any question I needed to ask, I would go to the warehouse.

I started paying more attention to what clothes I wore and how I looked when I went to work. I was slender with wavy brown, shoulder-length hair and wore fitted jeans, tops flaunting my small bustline, and stylish high-heeled clogs. As I walked into the warehouse, my heels announced my upcoming arrival on the cement floor.

I asked him about his life, and he asked about mine. I shared, "I'm living with my boyfriend, but things aren't going well. He's seven years older than me, and I don't feel the same about him as I did before. I was young when we first started going out and now, I feel like I'm looking for someone with more common interests and goals. He's an artist and he doesn't take care of himself. His mom still does his laundry and buys groceries for him. At his age he should be taking care of those things for himself."

He replied, "I'm kind of laying low these days, tired of the bar scene and all the trouble that goes with it. I just hang out at home most of the time."

There was something about him that I was attracted to. I felt comfortable, just sharing how my day was going or what my plans were for the weekend.

One day, I decided to ask him to join me for lunch at one of my favorite places. We went to Eastern Style Grinders at Golf Mill Bowling Alley about 15 minutes from work. They had great hot sandwiches with all the toppings.

He asked me out for dinner a week or so later. I was still living with my boyfriend, so I had to make up a story about going out with friends after work. I never liked being dishonest, but I had to figure out what my next step would be. Would I move back home? Could I move back home? I'd have to ask my parents.

We met at The Steer & Stein, a casual but nice, steak and beer restaurant in Chicago. I usually had a pretty good appetite, but this time I couldn't eat. Our conversation was easy, he listened attentively and looked at me adoringly, as I spoke. I was also interested in what he had to say and how he felt. I could be honest and open about what I thought.

I realized my living situation would have to change, but it would take time and effort. I was falling for him. After dinner, we met at Hala Kahiki for drinks. We shared a Tropical Volcano Drink, sipping from two straws gazing into each other's eyes across the table. Buzzed from love and alcohol, we stumbled out the door to my car to say goodbye.

He leaned over and kissed me. I went along enjoying our first kiss, embracing him tightly in this forbidden romance. We knew we shouldn't have been together yet, but it happened.

"I'm not sure what I'm going to do. I really like you a lot, but I feel bad about my boyfriend. I think I'm going to have to move back home. I have to tell him."

"Whatever you think is right, I'll support you," he said. "I want to be with you, but it's up to you to make that choice."

I didn't realize how much my moving out would affect my boyfriend, but it did. He was taken by surprise. He was in his own world with his art and friends, so he didn't realize I was growing distant. I assured him he would be fine without me. He would have more time to focus on his art.

I knew in my heart that I wanted to be with Randy now. I talked about my family and prior relationships, and he understood and encouraged me that I was "normal." He made me feel good about myself even though I made some careless mistakes in my life. His sensitivity to what I needed to hear was amazing.

I moved back home with my parents. Luckily, they were okay with it. I think they were concerned about me, living with this older man and happy I was going to be home again.

We spent a lot of time together, during and after work. We went walking together in the forest preserve and had romantic picnics. The big rocks overlooking lake Michigan in Evanston was another spot we liked to spend time. As we strolled through Brookfield Zoo holding hands, we first exchanged the three words. "I love you." Everything felt comfortable when we were together.

Sitting in his two-tone brown Chevy in front of my parent's house, we often talked until the golden sun rose above the distant horizon. I would go inside to sleep for a few hours and get up and go to work.

We spoke about our religious beliefs that we grew up with. Randy was raised Catholic and made his First Communion and attended Church regularly, but at this point, he claimed he was agnostic. He didn't believe in organized religion as some of the rituals didn't make sense to him. We both questioned our prior faith now, seeking what we felt was our truth.

One night he opened his heart to share about how he had lost his brother several years before to Lupus. "I really miss my brother. Sometimes I can't believe he's gone."

"I'm so sorry. You must have been devastated."

"He had two young kids that I was close with also, and I never see them."

"Why, what happened?"

"He and my parents were fighting before he passed, and now his wife won't let them see their grandkids. It's a mess."

"Wow, I'm so sorry. That's awful."

"He made his wife promise to not let them see my parents."

"That's too bad. It sounds like he wasn't thinking clearly. Was he mad at you? Maybe you can reach out to his wife to arrange something to visit them."

"I don't think he was mad at me, but I feel bad for my parents. They lost their son and their grandkids."

"Maybe you should try since it's bothering you. His wife might be happy to hear from you. She lost her husband. She must be devastated."

We spoke many times about this sad situation, and eventually he did visit the kids, and we attended some of their birthdays and graduations.

His whole family struggled with the loss of his brother in many ways. I felt his heart when he spoke about this situation and sensed the sorrow it caused. His big brother was gone from his life. There were five sisters between the two of them. He idolized his brother as a young boy, having special memories of the time they spent together. His sensitivity was endearing to me.

Rodeway Inn on Cumberland in Chicago turned into our place to be together most Saturday nights. We checked in with our stash of pot, champagne, beer, snacks, Newports, and my sexy nighties. We ordered room service, so we didn't have to go out.

The Wyndham Hotel in Skokie was another place we liked to stay. They had a restaurant on the top floor that made the best Beef Stroganoff. One time we waited too long for the waiter to bring the check, so we dined and dashed back to our room. Our life at this time consisted of sex, drugs, and whatever we felt like doing in the moment.

Another side of our relationship was seeking peace from within. We had a mutual friend at work named Shoji. We spoke with him a lot about a spiritual practice that he followed which was based in Japan. He wanted us to meet his Japanese friend Kyoko who gave advice to people from her spirit guides. Kyoko and Ike, her husband, also studied under the guidance of Tomekichi Taike from Japan.

Kyoko had sparkly brown eyes, dark curly hair, and a bright smile that melted my heart as soon as I met her. I was both curious and anxious about what she might say to us. Her husband, Ike appeared to be a gentle man taking care of their three young children as we spoke.

Kyoko looked at Randy and I smiling warmly and spoke in Japanese as her husband translated to us.

"You will have a lasting relationship and create a beautiful family. You have been together many times in the past and have a mission to complete this lifetime," he shared.

Tears welling up in my eyes as I looked at Randy. "Thank you," we both said as we bowed towards her.

They lived in a small, simple apartment full of joy and laughter. We were grateful we had the chance to meet them.

Even though we were young and had lots of growing up to do, there was always a strong spiritual interest underlying in our relationship.

Realizing we were spending too much money on hotels and room service, Randy decided to move out of his parent's house and get an apartment. We planned and cooked meals together, and I spent weekends there, but I didn't want to move in totally.

When I had moved in with my prior boyfriend, I was curious how it would be to have the freedom away from my parents. Things were different now. I only wanted to move out when I was sure I wanted to be with someone for the rest of my life.

After a year or so of care-free living, we were jolted awake with a pregnancy scare. We weren't ready to have a baby but realized it could happen easily. Shocked by the possibility, we knew change was needed.

"Maybe it's time we think about getting married. We love each other and spend a lot of time together, and I don't want to just move in. What do you think?" I inquired.

"You're right. I love you and want to be with you. Let's get married," he agreed.

Randy saved up for a couple weeks to buy a one fifth of a carat diamond ring at Service Merchandise. Kneeling in front of me as I sat on the rose-colored sofa from his aunt, in the living room of his apartment he proposed. "Will you marry me?"

"Yes, I'd love to!"

We were married June 6, 1982. I was twenty, and Randy was twenty-one years old.

After getting married we began to settle into more of a routine of working, creating a home for ourselves and a stable future together.

My sister had a baby named Valerie. I adored her. I spent a lot of time with my sister, her baby, and my mom. Randy was making good money at Nestle USA, so we decided it would be a good time to start a family.

What Do We Do Now?

♥

On June 23, 1984, our first son, Alexander Randolph, was born. Parenthood was an awakening for both of us. We were the youngest children in our families. We didn't have a lot of childcare experience.

Our first born wasn't at all what we expected. The birth didn't go as planned with the Lamaze practice we learned about. I had over twelve hours of labor, and an epidural and forceps were used for delivery. Alex had jaundice, so I couldn't breastfeed since they wanted to flush the jaundice out with formula and keep him in the hospital for a couple of days before I brought him home.

Sometimes things don't work out as planned. I had to trust the medical professionals to make the best choices for my baby. Although I was disappointed, my priority was having a healthy baby and safe birth.

After finally bringing him home after a few days we were intimidated. "What do we do now?" We looked at this helpless newborn baby lying in the white bassinet in front of us. He must have sensed that we didn't know what we were doing.

He cried and cried and screamed and cried for the first three months of his life. "Maybe he's wet. Is he hungry? Does he have gas?" We'd go through the check list and try everything we knew to soothe him.

My *Dr. Spock Book for Baby & Childcare* was my only hope: Put the baby out in the sun for a nap, it said. Take the baby for a walk in the buggy or car ride to calm him down. Sometimes the sound of the vacuum helps. After reading about the vacuum, I found something easier to use.

"Let's try having the hairdryer on the desk. Maybe it will calm him down hearing the sound." There were no white noise machines or mobile phones, let alone apps, in 1984. None that I knew of anyway.

The hairdryer worked, and we finally got some rest. We were thrilled to discover this tool. We used it for a few months and wore out a couple of hairdryers, leaving it on for 20 minutes or so each time until he was asleep.

My sister's baby whom we saw frequently was very easily amused and calm, so we thought having a baby would be easy.

We grew up together as we learned how to take care of this totally dependent living being. We gave him baths in the sink. Randy would hold him around his abdomen, arms and legs dangling above the sink, and I would wash his slippery, fragile little body.

We fell in love with this baby as we nurtured and cared for him growing and changing before our eyes. His smiles, laughs and new triumphs of crawling, sitting, and taking first steps were our newfound joy. Our wild and carefree days were in the past now.

A friend had given us a joint, and we decided to try it the night before his first birthday. After a few tokes, I said, "I can't do this now. What if something happens to Alex, and we need to go somewhere? It doesn't feel right."

"You're right," Randy agreed. We flushed it down the toilet and haven't had any since. It was time to face our responsibilities as parents.

Almost two years passed, and we decided we would try to have another child. Nicholas was conceived quickly and born September 2, 1986. He liked to suck his thumb and comfort himself and didn't cry so much. Maybe we learned a thing or two from the first baby, but everything just seemed to go a lot easier.

Mother's Love

♥

L ife was getting easier with our two sons, and we started getting together with the friends from the spiritual study based in Japan. We started going to seminars with them out of state, bringing the kids and working on ourselves spiritually. From the beginning of our relationship, we shared the seekers mind. I enjoyed the community and continued my self-reflection through journaling. The focus of the study was to align with "Mother's Love, which is the same as God's Love."

Tomekichi Taike was the teacher of the group. He was a school principal for many years and guided people with wisdom from his awakenings. One day, he felt the overpowering love from his mother and awakened to the realization that her love was the same as God's Love. If we could resolve our relationship emotionally with our mom, then we could feel God's Love. I felt this truth in my heart and reflected on this daily to feel that genuine love. There were barriers to feeling this love for everyone individually based on their experience. This study was fairly new, and books were being written at the time.

I was home with my kids, so I was happy to help by translating books from rough Japanese translation to more understandable English.

Channeling people's hearts during meditation started to flow from me. "Channeling" is speaking someone's subconscious thoughts that sometimes they aren't aware of or maybe don't want to know about or admit to. I shared what I channeled with family members and friends. These channeled messages weren't always well received, but I felt the need to share them.

"I feel so lonely and lost. I don't know which way to turn. My body is so painful. Someone, please, help me." My brother's subconscious spoke to me. I wrote down what I received and gave it to him.

"JoAnn, what is this? I'm not sure what you're trying to do but leave me out of it." He was angry. We never spoke of it again. I knew it was true, but he didn't want to admit his weakness and suffering. He went through a painful divorce with two young children and passed away at the young age of sixty-two. He was very sick and never took care of himself.

I was always more interested in talking about feelings than most people around me, including my family. It made me sad, but that's the way it was.

Memories of a Past Life?

♥

During a deep meditation in one of the seminars in New Jersey, I noticed that my head started tilting to one side. I spoke to this past life "spirit." This spirit expressed feelings of loneliness because I didn't accept this broken part of me. It was a part of my past that I didn't want to acknowledge or love. I opened my eyes, my head straightened, and I felt like I met a part of me that I didn't acknowledge before.

I carried a lot of shame in this life for choices I made growing up due to my lack of self-esteem. I would need to address these choices to forgive myself. When the time was right, I would.

The spiritual group had a seminar in Chicago, and we invited everyone to our home after for dinner. Our Japanese friends from Chicago helped us prepare bulgogi beef, sushi rice and spinach gomae. Everyone enjoyed the meal prepared with our sincere effort.

"Mr. Takahashi wants to invite you to come to Japan with your family for a tour and seminar," our friend translated.

"We would love to go, but we don't have enough money," I answered.

"He will pay for everything. He has plenty of money," our friend answered.

"For all four of us?" I questioned.

"Yes, he will give me money to pay for your airfare, and everything will be arranged. The tour and seminar will be in two months from now. Book your airfare, and I will give you the money."

We couldn't believe this was happening, and I was a bit nervous thinking about the long trip. It would be a twelve-hour flight, then a layover for two hours before a short flight to land in Osaka where the tour was.

How would I manage this long trip with two young boys? Are we doing the right thing? How can we turn down such a great opportunity for our family? We have to do this.

A month before the trip, I wasn't feeling normal, "My period is late. I'm not sure what's going on. I'm feeling tired lately," I said to Randy. I was worried something was wrong. "I guess I better go to the doctor."

I was asked to give a urine sample and they took blood too.

"JoAnn, the results came back, and you are pregnant," the doctor stated.

"Oh my god, really?" That's the last thing that was on my mind. We were busy with the boys most of the time and didn't have a lot of "alone time" or energy for such things.

As soon as I got home, I called Randy. "I'm pregnant."

"That's great!" He was thrilled.

"How am I going to travel like this?" What am I going to do?"

"We'll manage. You'll feel better by then," Randy assured me.

"Okay, I hope so."

Travel was difficult with two young boys and being pregnant. When we arrived in Japan, the group welcomed us at the airport. We were driven to our hotel, which was a small room with two futons on the floor. The bathroom wasn't much bigger than the one on the airplane but there was a small shower. It was great to be there and on land. Laying in the bed that night, I still felt the vibration of the plane.

The tour started the next day. We had a busy schedule going from one city to the next by bus. Travelling by bus with the group, everything was arranged for us.

Some of the places we stopped at, only had the porcelain toilet seat on the floor, and we had to squat above the hole and make sure our pants weren't in the way. One of the resorts had temperature-controlled toilet seats and a bidet to spray after use. Reading the diagrams of which buttons to press to direct the spray in the right area was challenging but it was nice once I figured it out.

The countryside was beautiful just like I had seen in the movies. Mountaintops lined the distant horizon and rice fields scattered everywhere. Sheets rustled from the breeze on balconies, and small houses covered the hillsides. Small cars crowded the streets creating lots of hustle and bustle. Many people rode bikes and drove in alleys to get around the crowded streets.

The seminars were long days of lecture being translated for us from Japanese. We listened to people's past life experiences, their subconscious thoughts, and struggles through channelers.

Randy was touched deeply and shed tears at times. "This is amazing. I can't believe we're here."

I felt overwhelmed with worry about our young boys and was exhausted with my pregnancy and all the travel. The kids got antsy at times, playing, and coloring next to us while we tried to focus. Others from the group tried to help with the kids, but they were mostly staying beside us.

I made a call to my parents one evening. "JoAnn, is everything ok? How are the boys? Are you okay?"

"Yes, we're fine. I'm tired, but everything is ok. The country is beautiful, and the people are very nice to us. All the TV programs are in Japanese, though."

"Ok be careful and get some rest. I love you," Mom said as we hung up.

"Love you too," I answered as my jaw dropped. Tears flooded my eyes.

My mom never said those words to me as long as I could remember. They went thru my mind the rest of the trip, realizing how worried she must have been about me and my young family. I had longed to hear those words for many years.

One night while sleeping on the futons, the ground started to shake, and pictures on the wall and lamps on the tables began to wobble. Blaring horn sounds began to vibrate from speakers in the hallway, followed by Japanese gibberish. We surmised it was instructions that we couldn't understand. People were running thru the hallway, going somewhere for safety. We realized it was an earthquake but decided to stay put in our room with our young family, snuggling together in fear. Trying to stay calm to reassure the kids, we sang ABCs together to distract ourselves and them. After thirty minutes or so, everything quieted down, and people went back to their rooms. There was more ground shaking intermittently through to the next day, but it was not as strong. People just went on about their business as this was a normal occurrence for them. We were staying at Atami, near Mt. Fuji, which was affected by earthquakes frequently.

The trip was an opportunity of a lifetime for our family and the group was kind and gracious to us. We were grateful.

February 5, 1990, Teresa Joy, our surprise baby girl, was born.

We continued to meet with a couple from the group in Chicago for a couple more years. We were busy raising our family, so we drifted away from this group and some of its philosophy. It was difficult to stay in touch since they were based mainly in Japan. We were sad to drift away from this relationship, but we had to accept our situation. We also lost contact with the friend who had introduced us to the group. We had a family, and they did not, so our lives were different.

Do I Have To?

♥

A month after the car accident, my painful neck condition wasn't improving. I called my doctor, and he advised me to see a neurologist after hearing about my symptoms.

As an adult, my Christian Science belief was in the past for the most part, but I still had a connection to God. I prayed for comfort and answers. The answer was that I needed to go see a doctor to find out what was going on.

The neurologist's office was in an office building with large windows. The waiting room was formally decorated, and the staff was business like. Stepping into the room to wait for the doctor, there were hammer-like tools on a silver tray, lined with white paper, and diagrams of brains on the walls.

The doctor came in abruptly, "What's going on?"

I replied, "I was in a car accident a month ago, and a couple weeks ago I noticed my head starting to move to the side on its own. I feel like I have no control over my neck muscles. They are very tight and painful."

"Let's do a few tests." He used the small hammer and tapped different areas on my knees and elbows to check my reflexes. Then he had me hold my arms straight out in front of me while he tried to push them down, one at a time. My reflexes seemed responsive, and my arms were strong.

"It looks like Cervical Dystonia, otherwise known as Spasmodic Tor-ticollis," he said with certainty. "It is a neuromuscular condition stemming from misfiring signals in the brain. There is no known cure. We only treat the symptoms."

"Uhhhhh---." My jaw dropped towards the floor. "What could cause this? I can't believe it. I've never heard of it. Will it get worse?"

"It can come on from a head injury or a multitude of causes. It could get worse; each person is different."

Maybe it was from the physical and emotional stress of the recent accident. I couldn't believe how nonchalant he was. This was my body condition, and he acted like he was telling me I had an ingrown toenail.

My teary eyes glared at him in disbelief. Without batting an eye, he took out his prescription pad to write prescriptions. "These may help relieve some of the symptoms. They are used for Parkinson's and Multiple Sclerosis patients. They work to alter the brain to change the neuromuscular activity. They do have some side effects. You will need to take precautions while trying them. They could make you sleepy, so you shouldn't drive until you know how they affect you."

I was 35 years old, and I had three children to take care of and a husband. I couldn't be sedated and foggy headed taking these prescription drugs. This wouldn't work for me.

'Okay, aren't there any other options? Would physical therapy help?"

"Botox injections are used sometimes. There is research being done to see if they help."

I never even wanted to take medications for a headache. I would take one Tylenol first to see if it helped, and if I needed another, I would take the second one as advised on the bottle. As a child, we weren't given medication for anything. Even If I had a cough, my mom would give me a teaspoon of honey. She didn't have medications at home since she was Christian Science. She would study her lessons from the *Bible* and *Key to the Scriptures* when we were sick.

I picked up the prescriptions that were ordered, feeling numb and dazed. When I brought them home, I read the horrifying side effects and never took one of those pills prescribed that day.

The jerking motion from the van spinning around and the stress it caused must have caused this Cervical Dystonia to wake up in my neck.

I read about the possibilities of head injuries causing this condition. I suffered a couple incidents of being hit on the head. When I was eight years old, a heavy plastic suitcase full of papers and books fell on my head from a shelf in my closet. As a teen while cruising around with my friends, I fell out of the back of a van. This incident resulted in blood oozing from the back of my head and a painful lump.

My mom also had shaky hands as she was getting older, which I learned after some research was essential tremor. This was also a neuromuscular condition like mine. Some people would have these spasms throughout the whole body. I was lucky mine was only in my neck and shoulders at this point.

Could it get worse as time went on? I was haunted by this thought.

Sometimes fear and despair would take over my mind. I turned to my journal and wrote:

I may never be able to enjoy an active life with my husband. I'm afraid he will be bored and leave me. Will I get better and be able to do more activities without pain? Why is my neck so painful? Why are the muscles so tight and painful? Why can't I hold my head up straight? Why? I am angry with my condition. I'm angry my muscles are so tight and keep pulling and stretching my head into awkward postures. It's so painful and ugly. I look strange and feel constant pain unless I'm laying down. As soon as I get up the muscles squeeze and pull until I can't take it anymore and must lay down. Stop it. Just stop. I can't stand it anymore. I can't even sit up unsupported. The pulling won't stop.

I would speak to my pain: *Why are you doing this to me? What is wrong with me? Why don't you leave me alone? I hate you, and I hate what this is doing to my life. I hate the whole thing.*

I feel so angry and discouraged. I can't live like this. I have a family to take care of, and I can't do it when I'm in such pain all the time.

Gratitude would come through after releasing the fears and frustration: *I'm grateful for the things I can do. I can still work and enjoy visiting with family and friends. I can manage to do most things in my life, except physical activity. I hope someday I can do it again. I'm grateful for my life and the moments of joy. I'm grateful for my family to share time with. I'm grateful for my children to show me what I haven't realized. I'm grateful for adversity to help me appreciate the calm times. I'm grateful for moments to myself to feel peace within. I'm grateful to be at one with nature and hear the birds sing and feel the simplicity of life.*

I prayed: *God, please guide me and comfort me in my time of need. I feel so alone and lost. I am afraid to make things worse for myself and afraid of the suffering. It is so painful. I feel so helpless.*

Can I Heal Myself?

♥

Give yourself good news to make a good brain.

I was determined to find an alternative treatment for my condition. I did not want to take those prescriptions.

In our basement, there was a used computer from Randy's work, which Alex played video games on most of the time.

One night, I sat at the computer in the corner at the small desk for hours looking for any information on Cervical Dystonia or Spasmodic Torticollis. I waited and waited as the dial up internet service clicked and screeched its way to the websites I queried.

I had learned about Microsoft Office programs at work and their Human Resources software, but the world wide web was foreign to me.

I would go from one site to another, stumbling my way around, waiting for the information to load to find any information about holistic treatments or supplements for Cervical Dystonia or Spasmodic Torticollis. It wasn't a common diagnosis, so the results were scarce.

After hours of waiting and searching, I found a site called Spasmodic Torticollis Recovery Clinic (STRC) in New Mexico. "All right, finally I found some hope," I cheered as I opened my eyes wider and sat up straighter in the chair. Randy came to see what I was cheering about.

"Did you find something?"

"There's a place in New Mexico that this lady named Abbie runs who had the same condition. It's a whole program with exercise and diet. It costs $800."

New Mexico seemed so far away; would I have to go there alone?

"Wait! It looks like they have a long-distance program," I said. "They send the information, and I keep in touch by email. Can I sign up?"

"Of course, if you think it's a good idea. I want you to feel better, honey."

"Thank you. Your support means so much to me." I always felt loved and cared for by him. He did whatever he could do to help me. I was lucky to have such a loving man for a spouse.

This program could work for me. I would be able to ask questions and have assistance whenever I needed. Abbie ran the program and was a recovered Cervical Dystonia sufferer. She created this program based on her recovery that took years of hard work and trial and error. The program included special exercises, vitamins, diet modifications, and prayer.

I guess I always had a sense that there were natural ways to heal our bodies, maybe from my Christian Science background? This program felt right, so I ordered it right away.

There were some exercises and eating tips like cutting caffeine, sugar, and alcohol on the website, so I started with those the best I could. I've never been able to cut out sugar totally, but caffeine and alcohol weren't a problem since I rarely had them. Sugar is my only vice, but I did cut back some.

I watched for the mail every day for my videos and books to get started.

Package of Hope

I received the package with a notebook full of information and exercises to follow, a cookbook, and a VCR tape with exercises to follow and the massage technique. I followed all the directions as instructed to the best of my ability. I was going to get better just like Abbie and others that wrote testimonies about the program.

The main part of the program was getting the neck muscles to relax and come back into balance to support the head. This had to be done gently and slowly to avoid more spasms to the muscles, while also working on range of motion. If the muscles started to spasm more, I would need to back off. The exercises also focused on me trying to keep those neck muscles relaxed while I moved my body from a laying down position to kneeling and on my hands and knees and slowly standing up. I also followed the daily recommended gentle massages and muscle stretching. There was also the diet part and taking a daily high dose of special vitamins. Cutting back on sugar was still my biggest challenge. They also recommended a special massager to help loosen the muscles in the upper back, especially for those who didn't have someone to massage them.

Having a program to follow for my healing meant so much to me. Now I had hope that I could get my life back. I would have to devote a lot of time to my own healing, but I wanted to do this as naturally as possible.

I read the program thoroughly and did the exercises religiously every day. I had a space in our room with a mat I bought for my exercises. I used some stretching bands, a pole, and pillow for laying down to keep my neck relaxed. Some of the movements caused more spasms, and I'd have back off and do less of those. The instructions warned about this, so I was aware not to go too far or too fast.

"Sometimes it feels like my condition is improving, and sometimes it feels worse. I'm not sure if it's helping," I would share with Randy.

"Just do your best. That's the way everything is. Two steps forward and one step back."

When I was able to start getting up from the floor onto my knees without spasms, I was thrilled about the improvement. This was progress.

Randy was My Rock

♥

E very night before bed, I sat in a chair in front of the mirrored closet doors in our bedroom as Randy massaged and kneaded the tight muscles in my neck. He would also hold the top of my head gently while I turned side to side, working to improve the mobility in my neck. Holding the top of my head was a sensory trick to help balance my head easier. Even if he was exhausted after a long day at work, he was willing to massage my neck for me.

"Are you ready for your massage?" he would ask.

Sometimes I was tired and just wanted to go to bed or I knew he was tired. "It's okay. We can do it tomorrow."

"No, let's do it for a few minutes. I want you to get better."

"Thanks, honey, for all your help."

He wanted more than anything for me to feel better. He took over doing laundry and much of the household chores since I was so desperate. I still cooked most of the meals since I was home earlier. I would rest first when I got home from work, ice pack around my neck to ease the pain while sitting in my beige leather recliner with the high head rest. When it was time to start cooking, I would leave the ice pack on while I prepared dinner for my family.

Workdays were long and almost unbearable, sitting supported at my desk as much as I could. Getting up for any reason was treacherous. All I wanted to do was go home after work to my ice pack and bed or comfy chair. If the kids needed a ride or something after work, I begged my way to get out of any extra obligation.

"Can your friend's parents drive you? I'm not up to it. I'm sorry."

"Ok, I guess I can ask," they would answer.

I felt bad, but I was desperate. Everything became about my pain, recovery, and limitations. I spent many afternoons in tears after getting through my day at work. I was in constant pain unless I was resting flat on my back or sitting supported in a chair.

Grocery shopping was painful also. Lifting and walking around the store unsupported was miserable. I shopped when I had to, but Randy did most of it. Being the kind man he was, he never complained.

I felt helpless and guilty, besides being in so much pain. My responsibility was to take care of my family, and I couldn't.

"I'm sorry I can't do more. I feel awful you have to do everything," I would say.

"It's okay. You'll get back to it when you feel better. Don't worry about it."

Before this happened, we loved to go for walks after work. We would unwind and talk about our day. I was in so much pain I couldn't go anymore. I would lay in my bed crying with frustration and sadness while he walked alone. This was very difficult to accept; how limited my activities and life had become due to this horrific, painful condition.

We had been married for 15 years and spent most of our time together. We had a happy life. He always helped with household chores and the kids when he could, but now he had to do a lot more.

Getting My Life Back

♥

I became the master of my circumstances instead of the victim.

After a year or so of daily practice I started to feel definite improvement. "Hey, I must be getting better," I said. I'd just realized I was not holding my head all the time to push it towards center. Tears flowing, "I can't believe it," I exclaimed one morning while pouring Cinnamon Toast Crunch for Teresa.

"Mom, yes, you look better. I'm so happy for you," Teresa answered.

Moments of joy came up randomly, realizing how far I had come and how great I felt.

Now my journal entries were filled with gratitude:

I'm so grateful to have my life back. I feel so much more alive now. I am blessed. Thank you, God.

Walking from my car to my desk, I took deep breaths and smiled to myself. Yes, I'm feeling so much better. I'm so grateful.

I offered to drive Alex and Nick to their friends or wherever they wanted to go. "Do you need a ride? I can drive you and your friend today," I would say happily.

One sunny afternoon after coaching Teresa's soccer game, Randy walked towards me. I was sitting in my chair on the sideline.

"I am so grateful to feel better and be able to live my life again. Thanks for being by my side, honey. I love you so much," I said as I wrapped my arms around my loving husband.

"I'm so happy to see you smile again. I love you. I wouldn't want to be anywhere else. We're a team," he replied, squeezing me tightly.

For Sale at Kohls

♥

I shopped at the Kohls Department store near my house. They always had sales and coupons to encourage a visit. Shopping was always a favorite past-time for me, looking for something to fill the void I used to feel. I was browsing the jewelry section this rainy Saturday afternoon, and there was a woman nearby coughing a lot.

My immune system was weak. I would get sick frequently since I wasn't able to manage stress well.

This woman coughing uncontrollably stood out in my mind especially when a few days later I began this constant cough. My throat was itchy, and this coughing reflex wouldn't stop. I couldn't even stop coughing to eat. Randy went to get soup from anywhere I would ask, to help quiet this cough. I tried cough medicine, cough drops, and teas. Nothing was helping.

I went to the doctor, and he gave me an inhaler and meds for asthma to treat the symptoms. I kept hoping things would improve, but they didn't.

Poor Randy was trying to sleep next to me while I was coughing most of the night. This went on for a few months.

One night I woke up from a sound sleep gasping for air. I was able to get back to sleep but realized I needed to go to the emergency room the next day to find out what was really going on. The combination of this cough and the inability to breathe in the middle of the night was too much.

Morning came, and I went to the emergency room to find out what was going on.

Perched on the end of the paper-covered bed surrounded by white curtains, the nurse inserted a long q-tip into my nostril. I felt the tip touch my brain at the top of my sinus cavity. As she pulled it out, my eyes watering and sinus throbbing, I gasped.

"I need to set up a bed for JoAnn Dickson in Intensive Care," I overheard through the curtain.

My heart raced, and my body began to tremble.

The nurse came back and took my water away, informing me, "The doctor said you should stop drinking liquids."

I was wheeled through the corridors and on the cold elevator to Intensive Care. Randy was holding my hand, shuffling along. The room was full of stainless steel and monitors and wires. There was a toilet a few feet from the bed with no door around it. Nurses were racing around hooking me up to the machinery as my heart continued to race.

Next, the Ear, Nose, and Throat Doctor came in to accost me. This time, the instrument reminded me of tampons on a string. The tiny tampons and string were shoved into one nostril and came out the other. "Don't swallow," I was told.

I squeezed Randy's hand, trying not to swallow or gag with this object dangling in the back of my throat. After two minutes of eternity, the objects were retrieved back through my nostrils, and my body sank in relief.

The results of the torture test were inconclusive, but they saw there was extreme inflammation in my throat and larynx, which was causing my nighttime episodes of waking up, gasping for air.

A couple days later, the results came back positive for Whooping Cough. After two days in ICU, they moved me to a regular room. The room had Quarantine Warnings on the door, and visitors had to gown up before entering my room.

Since I was Christian Science growing up, I never received any childhood immunizations or booster shots, which would have included "Pertussis" or Whooping Cough.

They started me on Intravenous antibiotics and Steroids to reduce the swelling to improve my condition; however, my uncontrollable cough, sometimes to the point of gagging, and my gasping for air in the middle of the night remained.

I would press the button to call for the nurses, and by the time they came in, I was settled down, trying to rest again. Now I didn't have Randy beside me to comfort me when I woke up at night, gasping for air. I missed him terribly.

Each night, I would hope and pray that I could sleep through without waking in terror, trying to catch my breath. I was exhausted between the coughing and not sleeping well. I was in the hospital taking medications to improve my condition, so it had to improve eventually. How much longer would it take?

An Angel Named John

♥

T he waking terror happened again, but this night John, a male nurse, appeared in my room when I rang the bell as I had done the nights before.

He held my hand gently and told me, "If you tense up when this happens, the episode will last longer. If you relax, it will pass faster." I immediately understood what he was saying. I took a deep breath and let this awakening sink into my body and mind. Now I understood how to get through these times with confidence. He gave me the power to control my body and mind. This was a huge awakening for me to realize my own ability to change the outcome of the situation by turning my focus inward.

This advice came straight from heaven to answer my prayers, and this man was the angel that delivered the message. My dear mother-in-law, whom I was close to, had passed recently. I felt her presence at this time. Being so desperate, she had sent this kind man to help me with this simple message.

This advice helped me with my whole outlook about this terrifying occurrence. The next night, if it happened, I could accept the situation easier and just let it pass. This gave me peace of mind.

I was overwhelmed with gratitude for John. I never saw him after that night. I asked the other nurses about him, and nobody knew who he was. They said maybe he was a floater from another area filling in that night. After I was released from the hospital, I sent an email to the hospital giving praise to John for his compassion. I never received any response.

Did he really exist or was he an angel sent to help me in my time of need?

My primary care doctor had come to check in on me. I was quite disappointed with him. He did give me antibiotics a few days before this happened but never tested me for Whooping Cough. In Chicago, there had been an outbreak of the disease that year.

I was in the hospital for a full week. Nobody visited me besides Randy. People were afraid to visit with the threat of this contagious disease. My children were already exposed, so that was a worry also.

I returned to my home; however, these nightly gasping episodes continued. Now I had the ability to manage them and let them pass. This advice was the most valuable tool that I received during my hospital stay. The episodes continued for two weeks, since my larynx had been so inflamed from the constant coughing, but Randy was next to me, and I now had the calm mindset to manage them. They became much less frightening.

Recovery was long, taking steroids and other meds to reduce the inflammation in my throat. My voice was nonexistent. Without much communication with others, I felt out of touch with the outside world. All I had was my thoughts and my inner world.

I journaled searching for some peace for myself, writing down my thoughts and worries during this tumultuous time. Life was happening without me; I had been suffering with this constant coughing for so long. I couldn't attend in any of the kids' soccer games, basketball, or even some meals with my kids.

I was missing work also, and those relationships. I had tried to go in even though I was coughing, before going to the hospital. I was hoping the distraction might help, but it got worse. The public health department notified them of my diagnosis, after I was hospitalized and the people that worked close to me had to be tested.

The effects of this disease weakened my body, and it took a couple months to fully recover. My throat was sensitive to choking for six months after.

After recovering from Whooping Cough, I changed doctors.

The Return of an Old Friend?

♥

If you choose it, it will happen; I will get better again.

A ll the trauma in my mind and body from the whooping cough and medications to heal, caused tight muscles to come back in my neck and shoulders. It felt like a familiar friend coming to visit again. I was aware that the muscles were starting to tighten and pull again, so I tried to rest more and do the muscle stretching exercises more.

"Can you massage my neck for me? I feel like it's getting tense again," I started to ask Randy again.

At least I wasn't coughing like before. I could get back to work and life now but with my old familiar friend Cervical Dystonia.

Using ice packs, my hand for support, ibuprofen and Bio Freeze for pain, I managed it once again. After all I had been through this was familiar.

"JoAnn, are you up for a walk tonight? It's a beautiful night," Randy would ask.

"Sure, let me put on some Bio freeze, and I'll get my shoes on," I would answer.

"Let's go out to dinner tonight. I have a taste for fish at Jameson's. Are you up to it?"

"Yes, just grab my cushion for me. I'll be ready in a few minutes."

I had a high back chair rest that I carried with me wherever I went. This cushion that could be strapped onto most chairs was recommended by the STRC program. I had one of these tall blue cushions at the office and at home. When I went for visits at friends' houses or even restaurants, I brought one with me. It began to feel like part of me. This blue head rest cushion made my life bearable. I even took it on airplane trips.

For the most part, I accepted my condition and went on about my life the best I could. What would the alternative be? I couldn't stay home all the time. I needed to live my life.

"Focus on what you can do, not what you can't do," from *Living with Chronic Pain* by Jennifer P Schneider MD PhD. This message touched me deeply. I share these words of encouragement to many who are suffering with chronic pain or illness.

I would also tell myself; I will get better again. I did it before, and I'll do it again. I will get better. It takes time and effort.

Stress Management

♥

L ooking back, I never learned to manage stress. My body was affected by the stress I carried. The muscles in my neck and shoulders were affected most. This was why smoking pot was so attractive to me. It helped me relax. There wasn't much talk about stress management and how we could help ourselves by learning breathing techniques and meditation to calm the nerves.

I searched for holistic ways of healing. I took supplements, drank relaxing teas, and tried to manage my stress, but these were never enough. I was also doing some of the exercises from the STRC program. It wasn't helping this time,

The thought of Botox injections started to seem more attractive. Maybe it was time to try those? I tried one more thing first.

Chiropractor Visit

♥

I went to a local Chiropractor, hopeful that he could help me. After a few visits for cracking adjustments, my head started to tremble like I had tremors.

I was beginning to learn to live with the tilted head, but the addition of the tremor was too much to bear.

After a month or so, the tremor subsided thankfully, but my original head tilt remained along with the painful muscle spasms. I was relieved, once again, with the old familiar condition.

It's amazing how we can get used to living with chronic pain. I would never go to a Chiropractor again after this experience.

Botulism Shots

♥

The only other treatment for CD was Botox injections. Botox is a type of drug called a neurotoxin. It works by stopping the nerves from functioning. On occasion, Botox may spread from where it's injected to other parts of your body. This can result in botulism, a serious condition that may cause lack of energy; difficulty breathing, speaking, or swallowing; drooping eyelids; double vision; hoarse voice; loss of control of your bladder; and muscle weakness. Botulism can occur hours, days, or weeks after the injection. In rare cases, the difficulty breathing, or swallowing can be life threatening. People who already have trouble breathing or swallowing may be at a higher risk for these problems.

Yikes! Would this be better or worse than medications that made me doped up and foggy minded? Should I suffer with this painful condition or try this therapy that could help but also cause botulism or being poisoned, also including the inability to swallow for 3 to 4 months?

I had been working and taking care of my family while in constant pain, so I had to do something. I used pain patches, topical creams, ibuprofen, magnetic wraps, and muscle relaxants. I would take the muscle relaxants before bed and pass out, hoping the effect would continue through the next day. I'm not sure about the muscles, but my brain was foggy the next morning.

I had to trust my instincts and try it now.

I made an appointment with a neurologist who had special training to administer Botox for movement disorders. He was in demand, so I had to wait two months for my appointment. This was a newer therapy, and at that time Botox wasn't available for cosmetic use like it is now.

The shots had to be given at least three months apart since this is how long the muscles would be affected by the Botox. Since these muscles that would be injected with this poison were close to the throat, swallowing could be affected for this long as well.

I was frightened of the outcome since it would last 3 to 4 months. My condition could become worse. I could feel sick, or I could lose the ability to swallow for a few months. The reality was poison would be injected into my muscles, which would travel also into my bloodstream.

I couldn't think too much about the possible side effects. I had to trust this was going to help. The first time or two might be ineffective, since they had to start with a small dose to see how my body reacted. Then I would have to wait 3 months until getting another set of injections. I was a guinea pig with no other choice at the time.

The day of my appointment arrived after lots of anticipation. I was led by the nurse into a sterile room with some machinery that was unrecognizable. She took my blood pressure and temperature to make sure I wasn't sick. She asked about my condition. "How long have you had Cervical Dystonia?"

"A couple of years, but it did go into remission for a while after doing a Holistic Program. Then it came back stronger," I answered.

"Let go of your head and put your hands down. Just let your head do whatever it naturally does so I can see the position," she instructed.

"It's so painful. I always want to support it."

"We must see the posture to figure out where the injections should go. It will just be for a couple of minutes." She took notes and marked my skin with a pen on the muscles that were spasming most. I let my head tilt to my shoulder and twist forward.

"Are the shots painful?" I asked. "I'm pretty nervous."

She reassured me, "The doctor has been using this Botox injection procedure for a few years now for Dystonia and other neuromuscular conditions and movement disorders. The results have been promising.

It will take about 10 minutes total. I'll be here with you. Just try to relax and breathe. You'll have to stay still for the injections."

She then began preparing me for the injections with cold alcohol wipes cleaning my skin around the muscles in my neck. The doctor would first use a machine to find the most active muscles with a needle and then inject the Botox into them as indicated.

The doctor came in and began to prepare the Botox shots by emptying the solution from the refrigerator into the vial with the needle on the end. The needles were about 2 to 3 inches long from my quick peek. I always looked away when getting blood drawn or any uncomfortable situation such as this with a needle.

The first part with the needle and the machinery checking for the active muscles seemed like eternity, but the injections themselves were quick. They injected four different areas to relax and balance the muscles that held up my head. The feeling of the needles going into the rock-hard muscles was a welcome release.

The doctor told me in a matter-of-fact tone, "There are many muscles in the neck, and they have a big job to hold up the head, which is like the weight of a bowling ball. It's amazing when they can work together to support the head properly."

I could breathe easier once the needles were out and my neck was wiped clean. Now I would pray. Within a week or so, I would find out if they helped at all, and if I felt any of the side effects.

Over the next few days, I did feel more tired than usual and a bit queasy but not too bad. This first set of injections, however, didn't affect my condition at all. I would have to wait three months to get more injections, and they would have to increase the dose to see if any improvement could be made.

The first doctor wasn't personable, which always meant a lot to me, so I was ready to try someone else. I was able to find other doctors who did Botox injections, and they didn't use the machine to locate the affected muscles. For the second set of shots, I tried a different doctor. There would be less poking and pain since he didn't use the machine.

This doctor had high recommendations in this Movement Disorder Neurology field.

My records were sent to the new doctor, so he knew the dosage I was given before. He could tell which muscles to inject from his own senses and experience. This time after the injections, I started to notice a difference in my condition.

At last, my pain was less, and the muscles were starting to relax after the injections. My head still tilted but not as severely. Life got a little easier. I could get back to some things like walking comfortably with both hands at my sides and visiting with friends and family without severe pain.

As the three-month mark got closer, the Botox started to wear off. The pain and stiffness started to come back. I could only get these injections every three months. I continued for a couple of years with this routine until one time after receiving my shots something different happened.

A few days after the shots, I started noticing that I was having trouble swallowing. I would have to swallow four times to get water down. Eating was also challenging. I had to eat soft food, swallowing each small bite several times. This was frightening.

How long could this last? Should I go to the hospital? Will it get worse?

I called the doctor to let him know what was going on. "Next time, we won't inject the muscles near the throat. Eat small meals and drink slowly. It will pass eventually. Go to the emergency room if it gets worse," I was told.

I was able to manage at home, but it could have lasted for three months. Yikes, not being able to swallow was frightening.

The next time I went for the shots, I reminded the nurse and doctor insistingly, "Please don't give me any shots near the throat."

"Yes, I see that you had trouble swallowing on your records," they answered. Every time after that, I reminded them to be sure it didn't happen again.

After a few years of regular injections, since I was getting good relief, I decided to try to space the injections further apart to see how long I could go. This way I could take notice if my condition was better even without the injections. I eventually spaced them out to six months, then nine months and my condition was better. I took a break from the poison shots for a while and would get prescriptions for muscle relaxants to use, to keep the muscles relaxed in between.

I was beyond grateful to feel some relief so I could start to live my life again. I could enjoy long walks with Randy and the kids and even started riding my bike again.

If you've never suffered with chronic pain, you have no idea what it's like to just feel normal.

She Couldn't Remember

I saw my parents every other week or so, and I called to check in on a weekly basis. I was the one to reach out to them. They never wanted to intrude. I always felt they weren't interested in my life, but they were busy living theirs, I guess.

I received a call from my dad while I was at one of Teresa's soccer games at Elk Grove High School. "Hi, Dad. What's going on?" I moved away from the crowd to be able to hear the conversation fully.

"It's your mom. I don't know what to do with her," he sounded upset. "She's not acting right. She forgets things and doesn't want to watch TV anymore or read. I found a couple bills that didn't get paid, and we almost had our gas turned off. I don't know what's going on with her."

"How long has this been going on? Something isn't right. You should probably take her to the doctor." My parents were always together, so naturally she was beside him when he called, hearing what was being said about her.

"Joe, who are you talking to? What's going on? I'm fine. Just forget about it." She was upset now.

"Let me talk to mom."

She said in a tear-filled voice, "I don't know what's going on. I can't remember things like I used to. The television programs aren't making sense. I don't know what to do anymore."

I did my best to console her. "It's okay, mom. It will pass. Everything will be okay." I was in shock and had my own fears about was going on. This was the first time I heard about any of this. My parents didn't share about things that were going on in their lives until it had been happening for a while, and the topic couldn't be avoided any longer.

My mom was always a very positive person. She didn't complain about much unless it was something that she couldn't ignore.

When I was growing up, she studied her bible lessons every day. If we were sick, she would sit in her chair and read more than usual to focus on the "right mind" to heal us with prayer. She would always say, "You know better," when we would speak of being sick. She sent us to Sunday School every week until junior high when we didn't want to go anymore, and she would attend church service every week. Her faith was a big part of who she was.

I frequently spoke to my siblings on the phone and saw each other for holidays at this time.

I called my sister, April, since she spoke to them and saw them more frequently to find out if she noticed anything and get her opinion. We agreed she should go to the doctor.

"Mom, we want you to feel better. The doctor can find out what's going on with your memory. Don't you want to feel better?" April and I lovingly encouraged her.

"Okay, I don't know what's going on. I can't remember things anymore. I used to pay the bills and read my books and now I can't do those things anymore." she tearfully answered.

My dad scheduled the appointment, and they went in. The doctor recommended a Cognitive Assessment. They would need to make an appointment to a special doctor for this test.

At the appointment, my dad told us about the questions they asked her. "Who is the president? What year is it? What is the name of the hospital we are in?" Unfortunately, my dad stayed in the room for her test so she would be more at ease. He said how he answered the questions for her because she didn't know them.

The diagnosis from the test came back: mild cognitive impairment.

My sister, my parents, and I went to a restaurant together for lunch shortly after this diagnosis. It was autumn, and my dad had a light beige jacket on, which he left on in the restaurant for a while before he warmed up.

My mom asked him, "Joe, aren't you going to take your jacket off?" A few minutes later she asked again, "Aren't you going to take your jacket off?" In a few more minutes she asked again, "Aren't you going to take your jacket off?"

My dad took his jacket off to avoid the same question in a few minutes. He didn't understand what was happening to my mom, and he would get frustrated with her and tell her, "Behave yourself, Shirl." He thought she had control over her actions and words and could change her behavior.

Leaving the restaurant, I walked ahead with my dad. "There's something wrong with her brain, Dad. She doesn't know any better. You have to be patient. She's sick."

"Okay, I don't know what I'm going to do with her. I get so tired of hearing the same thing over and over. She's always asking about your brother David and why he doesn't come see her. I try to tell her he was just here, he's busy but she doesn't listen. She keeps repeating herself, over and over."

"Sorry dad, we'll talk to David. Just try to change the subject when she starts to ask about him."

My dad's pride and joy were his cars. He bought a new one every few years. He had Chryslers, Buicks, and Cadillacs. The only difference I noticed was the colors. He spent a lot of time cleaning and waxing them on a regular basis.

They loved to go for a drive and would visit old neighborhoods in Chicago where they lived, go to the cemetery to visit their deceased parents and relatives, and go to restaurants for breakfast or lunch. At this time when my dad was having a difficult day with my mom, they would go for rides more frequently.

Olive Garden was a place they frequently went. She loved Noodles Alfredo so everywhere they went that was what she wanted. If a restaurant didn't have Noodles Alfredo, she was disappointed.

At home, she would voice her frustrations about people not visiting her and other complaints about not being able to do things as she had done before. She was used to being productive in the household, doing laundry, cooking, working on crossword puzzles, and watching TV. She would say, "Why don't they finish the TV programs anymore? I never see the end. I can't follow my recipes anymore or remember how to cook things I cooked for so many years."

My dad took over everything, not realizing she needed something to occupy her mind. I researched about Cognitive Impairment, which seemed to happen before Dementia. I found out patients needed to have something to do keep themselves active. I would suggest, "Have her fold socks or towels. Just let her have something to be responsible for." He would listen to what I said and not follow through.

I'm not sure if he didn't understand or he didn't want to face the reality of his wife being so sick. She had always been a smart woman. He counted on her to take care of the bills and money that he brought home for all their married life. My dad wasn't a great listener unless it was something that he was interested in.

During my weekly visits, I'd bring my dog, Mia; she was a cute lapdog that my mom enjoyed seeing. "She likes me," my mom said when Mia jumped up onto her lap. I would also play simple card games with her to increase her memory.

We would look at photos from the past, and I would listen to her stories about her sister Anna always being late. She would see her running down the street in her high heels to catch the bus for work. She also shared about being sheltered from a lot when she was young. Her and her twin sister Doris were the youngest. They didn't know their mom was sick with cancer until she was dying. She talked about her brother Paul who enlisted in the service because he didn't get along with his dad. Sometimes things didn't make sense to me, she would talk about an aunt like it was her sister and I would wonder what she was thinking or talking about, but I didn't question.

Her personality was different. She would speak up to my father more than before, which I was amused by. "Why don't you go wash your car and leave me alone," She would demand. My dad was always the outspoken one, so he was shocked by her outburst.

She was starting to stay awake at night and keep my dad up. The doctor prescribed medication to help her sleep. Then, she began to sleep later, and he would have to wake her. He was now responsible to make her breakfast, shower her, and dress her.

He was starting to look tired when we went to visit, and the house was dusty, and things were laying around which was unusual for him. He always prided himself with a clean house and car. He couldn't do what he wanted to since he was dressing, bathing, and taking care of her needs constantly. He loved her dearly and did what he thought was best for her. They had been together over 65 years now. He would never leave her side, but something had to change. We arranged for a caregiver to go to the house for a few hours twice a week.

My dad agreed to getting help, being exhausted with all his new responsibilities. The caregiver would cook meals and help my mom with her shower. My dad also enjoyed the visits with her since my mom wasn't much company for him anymore. My mom, however, didn't understand why this woman was visiting with my dad so much. My mom started to get jealous, feeling that this woman was interested in her husband. We felt good just knowing they were getting help. This was all we could do for now.

Just the Two of Us!

♥

And I'd choose you in a hundred lifetimes, a hundred worlds, in any reality, I'd find you and choose you.

The year was 2012 when the last baby bird flew from our nest, we weren't sure what we would do with our time and focus. We still had Mia, our light tan Cocker Spaniel, and Burton, a grey and white miniature rabbit. They were furry and cute but not the humans we cared for, worried about, and always considered for the previous twenty years.

We had our nine-to-five jobs and the responsibilities of taking care of the house, but something was missing. We weren't needed anymore. The kids had their own lives now, and we had to leave them to fly on their own.

Sitting on our deck and overlooking the yard and beautiful tree and flowers, we pondered like old people now.

"I can't believe the kids grew up so fast."

"It's unbelievable how fast the time went."

My mom always said things would change before I knew it, and now here we were.

We never truly understand what others say until we experience it ourselves.

Years before when our oldest was born, we needed to adjust to having another human in our lives to take care of. Now we weren't sure how we'd manage without the three of them.

We had our parents whom we visited on the weekends and a couple of friends to have dinner with and go away for weekends with.

I took a yoga class with the Continued Education Program for several years to get exercise and try to manage stress. By the end of class when were supposed to be resting, my mind was on to what I was going to do next.

I signed us up for Bridge Lessons, so we could have something to do as a couple. Randy wasn't thrilled with the idea. "Okay, are you ready to go for our first class?" I asked excitedly.

"Not really. I don't know why we have to do this. There's a Bull's game on tonight, and now I have to miss it because of this stupid class. Why don't you go by yourself, and I'll go next time?"

"This is for both of us. Why do you change your mind all the time after you said you would do something? I can't go alone. It's for couples."

He conceded, realizing he had to go. "Okay, don't sign me up for anything anymore. You go do your own thing, and I'll do mine."

We took the classes together and ended up meeting a lovely couple whom we continued to play bridge with and became good friends. This was how I tried to adjust to our empty nest, trying new things, and meeting new people.

Randy has a habit of resistance to trying new things and always ends up enjoying himself after I convince him to go along. It's just the way he is.

I Have What?

♥

Butterflies are God's proof that we can have a second chance at life.

J une of 2013, I went for my routine mammogram. I waited in the spa–like, large waiting room that was set up at Woman Care for the results just like all the other times I had been there. The nurse came back with a serious look on her face. My heart started to race; I was feeling shaky inside now.

"JoAnn Dickson, the doctor wants to go over your results with you." I followed her with my mind and heart racing. I couldn't feel my feet, but I kept moving.

My X–rays were on the screen in the dimly lit room, and he pointed to the X–ray pictures of my breasts. "This spot here looks to be abnormal. I'd like to take a biopsy to find out what it is. I'll write a prescription, and you can make an appointment for a biopsy. Here is the phone number. You can call the office to set up the appointment."

"Oh my god, I can't believe this. Can I wait? Is it urgent?" My voice started to tremble.

"It's best to find out early so we know what we're dealing with. I wouldn't wait too long."

"Ok, I guess I'll do what I have to do." A voice inside assured me it was going to be ok.

Leaving the Woman Care Practice that day, my inner voice began to speak loudly as panic wanted to take over. I took a few breaths and listened. I made a call to Randy and told him about the news and then said calmly that it would all be okay. I'm not sure where the inner strength came from, but it appeared when I needed it most.

I kept telling myself, whatever happens I will get through. I will cross the bridge if it comes up. Somehow, I felt a sense of strength and calm that whatever I needed to do I could get through.

I arrived at the doctor's office for my biopsy the week after my mammogram. Randy and the kids were deeply concerned, but hopeful it would all turn out ok. My breasts were small, and I couldn't feel anything, so I knew it had to be miniscule. Maybe it was a cyst. I tried to stay positive and kept telling myself I would handle whatever came up.

I was guided into a sterile room with a couple of nurses who prepared me and got the equipment ready for the procedure.

"JoAnn Dickson, come this way please."

"Can I use the bathroom first?"

"Sure, it's on the left, I'll wait for you in this room across the hall."

"Here's a gown for you. Leave the opening in the front."

"I'm nervous. Will it be painful?"

"I'll be with you. The area will be numbed."

The room smelled of sterile with stainless steel everywhere while masked and gowned bodies with long latex gloves and hair coverings moved about intentionally.

I sat on the edge of the table with white paper rustling beneath me. She opened my gown and rubbed the cold gel on my breast as I shivered with anticipation. As the doctor rubbed and pressed the ultrasound wand over and over the same area of my breasts, she held my hand. Finally, he found the tiny lump against my chest wall. The needle was inserted into my breast, and I felt stabbing pain, as he took a piece of the tissue. I couldn't believe I wasn't put to sleep for this awful procedure. It seemed inhumane.

After finishing the procedure, the gentle mannered doctor looked me in the eyes and said, "I think it is cancer." The test results would be back in a few days.

He was a kind man with a gentle mannerism, but these words frightened me to death. I couldn't believe this was happening. In the back of my mind, I knew it was cancer especially now. The inner voice came. I am strong, I'll get through this.

I was instructed to use icepacks and Tylenol for the pain. I did use the ice packs for a couple days for pain; the area was quite painful. It felt like I had been stabbed deeply into my chest wall.

For the next few days, waiting for the results, a sense of calm came over me about the situation. I was usually anxious about any medical stuff. An inner voice continued to guide me; I'll handle whatever I need to. If I must cross this bridge, I will. All is well right now.

Something began to shift in my mind. I felt the need now to enjoy each moment in my life. I didn't want to waste any precious time. I realized for the first time in my life, with the threat of this illness, how valuable every moment was. Randy & I went for walks after work, and I didn't have any complaints about anyone or anything. I was content with life.

I received the call a couple days later. "JoAnn Dickson?"

"Yes, this is her."

"This is Woman Care calling with your biopsy results. The biopsy was positive. We need to make an appointment for you to come in and make a plan with the doctor."

The doctor was a kind man and assured me he would take good care of me. "I will remove the tissue along with a margin around the cells to make sure we get everything. Once we get the biopsy after surgery, we will figure out what comes next. I will also take lymph nodes to test them to see if they are involved."

I was calmer than I would expect as he spoke. I listened and asked if I could wait a couple of weeks before having the surgery.

"My husband and son share a birthday, June 23rd. We go to Arlington Racetrack to celebrate every year with family and friends, and I'd like to go."

"Sure, that would be fine. The nurse will give you the phone number to schedule the surgery after the 23rd." He patted my leg and looked in my eyes. "See you soon."

The surgery was scheduled for June 27, 2013.

The next few weeks until the surgery, I was more present than ever before. I had no idea what my life would be like after the surgery. I would cross the bridge when I needed to, but I wanted to enjoy every moment. I appreciated my time with family and friends, laughed more and just relished my time.

I shared the news with close friends and family. "I'm trying to stay as positive as I can, so please don't tell me about anyone else's experience." Everyone understood.

My mom being Christian Science didn't like to talk about illness. She was not herself at this time anyway, but I shared briefly on the phone about my diagnosis. She said "You know better than that. Remember what you learned in Sunday School." My dad's response was, "Okay honey, good luck with everything."

June 27, 2013, arrived and Randy, my daughter Teresa, and my son Nick's fiancée Ashley were there before the surgery to support me. The Breast Cancer Center at Northwest Community Hospital in Arlington Heights was as comfortable as I could ever hope for. The rooms were spa like and bright. The staff was welcoming and compassionate. I felt the energy of their caring hearts. They asked about me and my family and husband as a friend would.

The preparation was like an assembly line. I was amazed how smoothly everything flowed. First, wires were inserted directly into the tissue that would be removed, which was detected by ultrasound. Then, the lymph nodes were marked that connected to that exact area that was affected. Everything had to be exact, and they had the right equipment and procedures to utilize.

I was amazed how succinct everything was. One of the nurses told me how common breast cancer was at that time, something like 1 in 3 women would have breast cancer. I was astonished by this fact. I

I HAVE WHAT?   87

thought, why is this so common? We must be doing something terribly wrong to cause such an epidemic.

This was the first time I would go under general anesthesia and have surgery, so I wasn't sure what to expect. I was calm, just trusting in the medical professionals that they knew what they were doing. I was brought to the surgical waiting area after saying goodbye to my daughter and daughter-in-law. Randy was able to come with me and wait while I was being further prepared. They covered me in a warm blanket and gave me something for my stomach in case the anesthesia bothered me. I urinated a few more times, which I do when I'm anxious. This was it. The time was here, and soon I'd be having a lumpectomy from my right breast. If they found something more when they started the procedure, they would need to do further tissue removal.

Randy held me tight as he wished me well. "I love you and we will get through this together. I'll be waiting for you."

The scent of sterile filled the room as I was rolled in on the paper-covered table. Stainless steel and bright lights were everywhere, as were several people in blue surgical gowns, masks, gloves, and head coverings. I felt like I wasn't present anymore. Just my body was there to be dissected.

The IV was inserted into my vein, and a mask covered my nose and mouth. The nurse instructed "Count down from ten."

"Ten, nine, eight, seven.........."

As I came back into my body, I felt as if I had returned from another place. I wanted to vomit but nothing came up as I heaved. The stabbing pain throbbed in my chest, which was bound tightly with a tube-top like bandage. As I moved carefully, adjusting my burdensome body, my brain continued to wake up. The room was spinning, and my eyes couldn't focus on anything. I kept my eyes closed as I struggled to calm my overwhelming desire to vomit and collect my awareness back into my body.

Randy was with me, and I could feel his concern, but I was still coming back. "Can I do anything for you, honey?"

"No, I'll be okay. I just need to relax."

The nurse came to check me each hour. "Are you ready to move now from the recovery area?"

"I'm still feeling dizzy and nauseous."

I stayed in the recovery area for as long as they allowed me. It was time to go to the area to prepare to be released. I was very groggy and dizzy and nauseous for hours after, not ready to get into the car. I sat in the chair, head in my hands, trying to settle and rest. Somehow, I'd have to manage the 20-minute ride home.

Teresa came in to see me, but I didn't want any visitors since I was so uncomfortable. She and her boyfriend Jon were supposed to drive us home, but I didn't want anyone else besides Randy to be with me because I felt so awful. I didn't want to vomit in front of anyone. They arranged things so Randy could drive me home as I wished. The ride was long.

When I got home, I went out onto the deck and sat in a chair soaking in the fresh air and breeze. I fell asleep for at least an hour until it was time to go to bed. The fresh air was a warm welcome after the tortuous day.

I always loved being outside in nature. As a child, my mom spent a lot of time on the back porch reading on our glider. I remember laying on her lap when I wasn't feeling well, being comforted in the fresh air. Having windows opened in the house always helped me connect to nature also.

We are part of nature, so being one with nature helps us heal!

My dad called me the next day to see how the surgery went. "Hi honey, how are you feeling?" His voice was caring and concerned. "Is everything okay?"

"Yes, it was a long day, but I'm doing okay. Thanks for calling. How's mom doing?"

"She's doing okay. She sits in the living room and looks out the window all day."

My mom's awareness was deteriorating, or she would have been the one to call. She had become a child, needing constant care and no longer the mom I knew.

I waited for the results from the biopsy of the lump, the tissue around it, and the lymph nodes they removed. The surgical wound was painful, and I had to keep my breasts bound in the tube-top bandage for a few days, icing the area, and rested a lot.

I went in two weeks later for my post-surgery checkup, and the doctor removed the binding and checked the wound, which was beginning to heal. Even though I had showered, I avoided the painful area, so the glue from the surgical tape was still on my skin. I didn't want to rub or disturb the area, so he removed the glue for me. I felt stupid but I didn't know what I was supposed to do, never having had surgery before.

He was pleased with the scar and the job he had done. He asked me to open my gown while sitting on the edge of the table. He looked at my breasts and commented, "They look pretty good; your nipples are even. Are you pleased?"

"Yes." One of my breasts wasn't as full as the other now, but that was a minor concern. The red scar was about 2 ½ inches long since they needed to remove a considerable amount of tissue to create a margin around the cancer site.

"I have good news about your biopsy results. The lymph nodes were benign. The cancer was Hormone Responsive, so we can avoid further growth by using hormone blockers. You will need to get radiation daily for three weeks."

"What about chemotherapy?" This was my main concern. I always heard about the horrible side effects, like nausea and hair loss and exhaustion, and I didn't want to go through that.

"No chemotherapy. I took out a wide margin around the tumor, and radiation will take care of anything else."

Phew, my breath became easier now, and my shoulders sunk down from my ears. I could handle radiation; chemo always sounded awful. "Thank you doctor for being so kind and doing all you have done for me."

He smiled gently, as he patted me on my leg. "You're welcome. The nurse will give you instructions about how to set up your radiation appointments. I'll see you when you're done with radiation."

I scheduled the appointments for my lunch time, so I wouldn't have to take a lot of time off from work.

I asked friends and family to take me to radiation appointments, so I didn't have to go alone and do all the driving. The trip was about 20 minutes each way, and the treatments were about fifteen minutes or so. Randy took me the most. Teresa took me a few times. My brother David, sister-in-law Cindy, and close friend Toni took me as well. I appreciated the time that everyone was willing to spend, and sometimes we went for lunch.

The conversations to and from the hospital those weeks were more honest. When we are faced with our mortality, priorities change.

"Honey, thanks for always being by my side. You mean the world to me. I know you're busy at work. I really appreciate you taking me. I love you so much."

"I love you too. I wouldn't have it any other way. We're in this together," Randy would say.

"Thank you so much for taking me, Teresa. It means a lot to me. I'm so glad I have you to support me. I know you have your own life now, and I want you to be happy."

Of course, mom. I'm proud of you and how you're handling everything. I know it's not easy. You've done many things for me and have always been there when I needed you. Sometimes I didn't appreciate you, I'm sorry. Now it's time for me to help you get through this. If there's anything you need, let me know."

My friend Toni was always checking on me with a phone call or text. Chicken rice soup was one of her specialties. She came to bring me the soup she had made special for me. Instructions on little notes explained exactly how to heat it up. With a warm hug as she was leaving, I felt her love. This soup warmed my body and soul. "I've been worried about you. I'm glad the surgery went well. Enjoy the soup and get some rest. I'll call you tomorrow."

"I know you were worried, thanks so much for the soup and your care. Our friendship means a lot to me."

She's one of those nurturing people that everyone should have in their life, and I love her dearly.

During the first visit for radiation, they made a cast for me to use during the treatments and marked the spots on my chest for the radiation to cover with a tattoo dot. It was the first tattoo I ever got! I laid on the cast in this MRI-like machine, and the machine went over the same spot back and forth for 10 minutes. The staff was very friendly, and I felt at ease after the first time because I knew what to expect.

Toward the end of the treatments, my nipple started to feel burned and very sensitive. I used pure Aloe Vera gel as recommended and a pad in my bra to keep it from rubbing.

The three weeks of visiting with my private chauffeurs on the daily trips to and from the hospital went quickly. On the last day of my treatment, I received a certificate from the staff that I completed the radiation. I was so happy to be done and grateful for their support, so I brought a box of Fannie Mae Candy for them. Medical staff make such a difference in these difficult experiences. I'm always grateful to have kind people taking care of me in my times of need.

A week after completing radiation, my friends and I went to dinner to celebrate finishing my treatment. I vomited that night, thinking this was part of my body's healing process after the radiation.

My sister-in-law Linda took me for my follow up Dr. appointment with the cancer specialist, since Randy had to be at work. I was grateful to have her company since it was a significant appointment. The doctor went over recommendations for prescription medication as a precaution, but with the help of my surgeon we agreed that my odds would be good to stay healthy without medication, if that's what I chose.

I was free to live my life again without interrupted lunches at work. I was able to walk around the outside track after lunch with Diane and Toni like before.

Gratitude was a big part of my journaling:

I'm so thankful for my health, my family and friends that helped me through breast cancer. I am amazed at how strong I felt as I lived through the surgery and radiation. Now is the time to enjoy my life and health.

"Let's go on a special trip to celebrate your health and birthday in August." Randy said.

"Sounds like a great idea. Let's go to Michigan. I love the sunsets over the lake." I was excited to plan our trip.

We enjoyed our time together like never before. Each morning we walked hand in hand on the sandy beach as the waves rolled in. When evening came, we sat on the beach to watch the vibrant, crimson sunset as it settled into the horizon.

Profoundly moved by nature's beauty, on the last breathtaking sunset on that trip, we spoke about what our priorities for the future were.

"I feel like I need to do something more meaningful with my life," Randy shared.

"I agree. We are so blessed. We have three wonderful children and a comfortable home and life. I want to be grateful every moment. We are so lucky to have each other for support. I love you."

"I love you." The energy of pure love, tingled through our bodies as we embraced.

In Sickness and in Health

September 2013, Randy started to notice more frequent urination and the inability to empty his bladder fully. He was waking several times in the night to urinate and wasn't getting much sleep with all the interruptions. This went on for a couple of months. He was hoping it was just a phase, but it got worse and worse.

He was on his way to work in Chicago when he called.

"I don't know what's going on. I had to get off the highway to find a bathroom, and I couldn't go. This is ridiculous. It's so uncomfortable. I need to get to the doctor. I'm coming home."

"That sounds awful. What are you going to do? I'll call the doctor while you're on your way back home." The nurse said he needed to see a urologist. I called one that was 15 minutes from home, and they squeezed him in.

He arrived home, his eyes looking of desperation. I never saw him this way. He dashed to the bathroom and tried to urinate again and only a drip came out.

That was the longest 15-minute drive to the urologist, as I watched him writhe and moan around in the passenger seat. He was usually the one driving, but I heard no protest this time.

We arrived at the doctor's office, and they took him in right away. I sat in the waiting room, worried sick about what was going on. He was my husband, best friend, and my rock.

Seeing him in this painful, vulnerable, weak state was heart wrenching. What would I do if something happened to him?

He appeared looking relieved and exhausted. They had to catheterize him to release the urine. After examination, the doctor said his prostate was enlarged and blocking the flow of urine. He would need to have surgery and further testing. Meanwhile they showed him how to catheterize himself until the surgery could be done.

I felt helpless and uncertain of what to do to help him. He spent long periods of time in the bathroom. I waited, sometimes in tears, trying to stay occupied and not be overbearing, praying he was okay, getting accustomed to this new way to relieve his bladder.

He went back to the urologist for further testing, including a blood test for Prostate-specific antigen (PSA) levels in his blood. The levels were elevated so he would need to get a biopsy of his prostate. They would go in through his anus to take specimens from the prostate. Another inhumane medical test he would have to go through for this enlarged prostate issue. I felt so bad for him needing to self-catheterize to relieve himself several times a day. It's amazing what people get used to doing as these kinds of problems arise.

Prostate surgery was necessary to reduce the size of the prostate. Early-stage cancer was detected and needed to be monitored with regular blood tests, but the real problem was the enlarged prostate blocking the flow of urine.

Our three adult children were in the waiting room with me the day Randy had his surgery. The surgery was to trim his prostate with a new turbo tool they were using. Once this was done, the prostate would no longer be blocking the flow of urine. There were other options such as total removal of the prostate, which he wasn't ready to do. There could be other unwanted side effects from total removal, such as changing his sexual abilities at the young age of 50.

Everyone said goodbye and wished him well as they wheeled him into surgery. My husband and their father, our pillar of strength, was now defenseless.

The surgery was done, and I could go see him in the recovery room by myself. As I walked back in through the doors following the nurse, I didn't know what I would see.

This was a man that supported me through childbirth, breast cancer, whooping cough, cervical dystonia, and other illnesses. He was my rock, and now I had to be there for him. I was scared to death about how I would be able to handle helping him with whatever he needed.

Laying in the bed, with tubes and IVs hooked up, was this man that I loved. He was moaning and writhing in pain. The nurse explained he was experiencing bladder spasms. This was a side effect after this surgery. They had given him meds, but they weren't working.

I held his hand and told him I loved him. Unable to maintain his composure he said I should go back to the waiting area.

He knew how I was with medical stuff and didn't want to be seen this way. Feeling powerless, I went back by the kids to give them the update. I told them about how uncomfortable he was and said they wouldn't be able to see him for a while still.

He was the one who stayed up through the night with my oldest son when he was vomiting all night when he was young. He was always there when any of us in needed care and compassion. Now we wanted to be there for him but there was nothing we could do.

After another hour in recovery, they brought him to a room where we could see him. We all went, but he was still in pain. I knew he didn't want them to see him this way so I said they should go home, and I would take care of him. A short time after they left, he said he felt nauseous, and I grabbed the tray to bring to him. He vomited into the tray, and I handled it with love and tenderness. He apologized, knowing it wasn't easy for me to handle. I reassured him not to worry.

I was grateful that I was able to stay strong and be there for him. When you love someone, you handle whatever you need to.

After he vomited, he was able to settle down and rest. The meds were starting to help the pain. I needed to be strong, and show compassion and care for him and somehow, I was able to nurture him as he had nurtured all of us many times in the past.

Going home from the hospital that night alone, it felt like part of me was missing. We were together most of the time since we were married, besides when I had the babies, and when I was in the hospital for other reasons. Our kids were all out of the house living on their own, so I was alone with Mia our sweet dog. She was my comfort that night, sitting on my lap until I was ready for bed.

The next day he was released from the hospital with a catheter, which would need to stay in place for two weeks. There was a bag attached to his leg containing the urine output, which was traced with blood. I was never the nurse type, but I helped him dress, trying to be gentle and unaffected. He was given instructions about emptying this bag and managing all that.

Crying to myself when he was in the bathroom for extended periods, I felt helpless. What would the outcome be after all of this? My husband, the rock in my life, was going through a trying time, and I needed to be strong for him. It was a long couple of weeks, with many extended periods of time in the bathroom. He was weary and anxious to get this object removed from his body.

He had the catheter removed and started urinating on his own again, which was uncomfortable at first, but things seemed better. He was off work for six weeks or so with all of this going on, adjusting to learning to self-catheterize and recovering from surgery.

After he had been back to work a couple of weeks, he was starting to have trouble urinating again. He had to go in for emergency surgery to see what was going on. The kids met us at the hospital, and we waited for the outcome, even more anxious this time. We thought the worst was over so what was going on now?

We were all in the waiting room, and the doctor called on the phone to talk to me after 20 minutes to our surprise.

When I went to receive the call, my oldest son, Alex, followed me, being there to support me. It was scar tissue rebuilding in his urinary tract, causing blockage again. Once I heard that everything was okay, I began to sob with relief, releasing emotion like a pressure cooker. The tears and sobs came out as I leaned on Alex's shoulders. I was so grateful to have my son there. This is a moment I will always remember. He was my rock when his dad couldn't be.

Thankfully the second surgery did the trick and he continued to improve after that.

We now had another reminder to be grateful and appreciate our life together and all our blessings.

Until We Meet Again

♥

"Don't be afraid of change; it's a beautiful thing," said the butterfly.

As time went on, my mom needed more care, and my dad had no time to do anything without keeping his eye on her. One day we heard from a neighbor that she was outside looking for her twin sister who used to live next door, but she had passed two years prior from Dementia. My dad was beside himself, not knowing what to do. He wanted to have her by his side but couldn't handle her care anymore.

We arranged for them to go to an assisted living facility together. They checked in before bedtime. When the nurse came to check on my mom, my dad thought they were invading their privacy. During their first night there, the phone rang. It was April. "JoAnn, I just got off the phone with the assisted living place. Dad called the police on them. He said they were trying to break into their apartment. Can you go there?"

"Oh my God. This is ridiculous. He doesn't understand. He won't listen to me. They will manage the situation. I don't need to get involved."

My dad took my mom home the same night they moved in, after all the arrangements were made for them to stay there together.

A week after my dad took her home from the assisted living facility our prayers were answered. My mom was admitted to the hospital with a urinary tract infection. Her care wouldn't be up to my dad any longer.

We begged for them to keep her there, since she wasn't being cared for properly at home. They eventually moved her to Hospice care. My dad could visit, and she was cared for properly. She was showing signs of stress and confusion with my dad dragging her around. We went to see her, and she was laying in the bed eyes closed, reciting the 23rd Psalm. "The Lord is my shepherd; I shall not want. He maketh me to lie down in green pastures: He leadeth me in the paths of righteousness for his name's sake. Yea though I walk through the valley of the shadow of death, I will fear no evil: for thou art with me; thy rod and thy staff comfort me. . ."

She was less aware of who we were and talked about her brothers and sisters more and parents as if they were with her.

My sister loved to bake, and my mom loved sweets. The second day of her hospice stay April brought some chocolate chip brownies. We all gathered in her room. Randy, my sister, and her husband were there with their two adult children. My mom ate three of the chocolate chip brownies, licking the chocolate off her fingers after she happily finished the last one. "Wow, you enjoyed those brownies, didn't you, mom? I can't believe you had three of them!"

"What was I supposed to do with them?" she answered boldly.

My mom acted like a little girl, thinking we were her siblings, "Why aren't Ma and Pa coming to see me?"

"They must be busy. They'll be here tomorrow." We tried to just go along with her delusions now. It seemed as if she was a little girl again, maybe going to see her family again in the afterlife.

That evening after we went home, my dad took her outside for a walk to the courtyard area, and they both enjoyed the fresh air. They sat on a bench and reminisced for a while just like old times.

The next day she was in bed, barely drinking anything, not interested in eating at all. She wasn't communicating anymore. She was winding down. It was time to say goodbye.

The following night, we received the call that she passed away. We went to meet my dad at the Hospice place shortly after. My sister, her husband Joe, and Randy and I were there. My recently child–like mother was lying lifeless in the bed. I was happy for her not suffering anymore, being dragged around by my dad, not knowing what was happening. I believe she willed herself to pass in desperation.

I touched her hand and kissed her cold forehead and said "I love you mom; you can rest in peace now. You were a good mom. Thank you."

My sister was speaking to the staff about what would happen next, and I was now in the room alone with my dad.

He sat by her bedside crying, "I can't believe it, Shirl, you said you wouldn't leave me." Holding her hand, he kissed her check. He turned to me and said, "I'll never forgive him. How could he do that to her? I'll never forgive him."

He was talking about my oldest brother, David. Their relationship was strained for a long time, and he didn't visit as often as my mom would have liked. She repeated over and over, "Why doesn't he visit me?" My dad was left to console her however he could.

He did his best to keep her happy, but my brother's visits were out of my dad's control. This must have been building in his mind for these last months, years, struggling with my mom's illness. Days before her death, my brother and his wife had visited her at the Hospice facility, and everything was fine. But after my mom passed, overwhelmed by her death, my father focused all of his anger on my brother.

From that point forward, he wanted nothing to do with my brother and his wife.

He refused to bring a picture of my brother for the memorial service. We went back to the house to get it. He never acknowledged them at the service or the luncheon after. We gathered as a family at Olive Garden about a week or so after the service, and he ignored them. A month after my mom's passing, everyone came to our house. My brother said hello to my dad, but he ignored him and his wife. This was the end of our family as we knew it.

I was relieved and happy for my mom. She was suffering and not living an easy life with dementia and the ability to function as she had before. I realize now my grief had to be postponed because I had to support my father and work desperately to mend my family.

My father was heartbroken after losing my mom. They had been married 65 years and together every day, minus a few hospital stays for births and surgery. They were attached at the shoulder. My Dad managed his grief by blaming my brother, which broke our family apart at this vulnerable time for all of us. Randy and I tried on several occasions to repair the relationship along, but it never happened.

After mom's death Journal Entry:

My father can be such a monster at times. I don't want to wake the sleeping monster, yet I don't know what to do. I know my father is hurting and so are we. We need to be together as a family, and he's stopping that from happening. I've resented him many times in my life, and now is one of those times. I don't want to make waves, but I am afraid of the consequences if I don't say anything. I want to be present without anger. My mother is gone, and I miss who she was before her illness. She wasn't angry or stubborn; she was honest and forgiving. He's being selfish. We need each other. I must be willing to stand up for what is right.

We had a family get together with my siblings, a few months after my mom's passing. My dad was invited but would not come since my brother David would be there.

While visiting on our deck, a beautiful monarch butterfly fluttered about, landing for a leisurely stay on some of us.

"It's mom coming to show us she's free now. All is well without her body." I expressed what I felt. Everyone was silent, enjoying the beauty of the butterfly.

My mom's passing brought me closer to her in spirit. She represented honesty, integrity, and forgiveness in my life. She wasn't strong enough to share her virtues outside the family. Looking back, I realize that's my purpose. I carry the torch of "Hope," my mom's middle name, forward.

Groupon for Meditation!

♥

Just when the caterpillar thought its life was over, it became a butterfly!

O ne summer day, about a month after my mom had passed, Heaven and Earth aligned, and a golden rope appeared for me to climb. I searched for this rope my whole life.

This golden rope came as an email from Groupon for an introductory session with Body & Brain Yoga Tai Chi in Mt. Prospect, Illinois. The ad included the word meditation, which is what I was looking for. I had to quiet my constantly racing thoughts. YouTube videos were okay, but I needed more. I attended a community church in the area for six weeks and could not find what I longed for. For 10 years I had also taken weekly yoga classes at a local high school as part of a Continued Education Program. It was summer break, and I was desperately searching.

A different church in the area also advertised a meditation class online and I went, and nobody was there. Someone in the building said it had been cancelled.

The day of the appointment arrived, anxious with anticipation, I arrived at Body & Brain Yoga Tai Chi. Mya, an Asian woman about thirty-five or so with long brown hair greeted me warmly at the door. Wearing a scent which smelled like comfort, her presence permeated my sinuses and heart as she hugged me.

I realized this was an interaction that I should feel uncomfortable with, but it felt natural to me.

She led me into a small room which had a golden large mat on the floor and soft lighting. There were beautiful wooden, oriental cabinets against the wall. On the wall was an Asian scripture with gold characters and a fancy gold frame.

"What brings you here today? Tell me about yourself and what you're looking for." She asked.

"I have three grown kids and a husband. Everything is fine there. My mom just passed away about a month ago, and the family has broken up. I feel very anxious about everything. My dad won't talk to my brother, and I'm not sure what to do about any of it. My mind is always busy. I'm looking for meditation and a way to quiet my mind."

She reassured me. "We can help you learn to calm your mind. I can tell by the way you speak, you're anxious about many things. I'd like to check your Chakras. Can you lay down on the mat for me?"

I laid down on the warm mat, resting my head on a small pillow covered by a paper towel. She asked, "Can I touch your chest and abdomen?" Resting her warm hands on my chest between my breasts, she said "I will check your heart chakra." She started to press firmly and speak gently to me. "How do you feel about yourself?" Tears flowed and sobs erupted from my body like an eruption of emotion that I had been holding in for a long time.

"I don't know. I try to be a good person for others, but I feel lost."

"It's okay, just let the tears flow. You're safe here." She softly spoke as she handed me tissues.

A warm, fuzzy feeling washed over me, as I wept with this total stranger. I felt loved and cared for unconditionally, as if I knew this young girl for many years.

I felt this was a safe place that I searched for my whole life. I could be accepted for who I was. Maybe I could get the help that I needed to feel better about myself and my life.

Once the sobbing slowed into sniffles she said, "Your Heart Chakra is blocked. You opened quickly with the tears. It is time to heal yourself.

You have come to the right place. We have a program of classes and workshops to help release more of this energy blockage and pain. I'll get the information to show you what I recommend for you."

She left for a few minutes, and I began to reflect on what just happened. The emotion swept over me so quickly, but now I felt at total peace.

She came back with the program information and pricing. The Groupon I purchased was $39, which included 10 classes or one month of unlimited classes. This is what I planned on doing when I came in. She recommended a package that included workshops and classes.

She advised me, "I recommend you come for classes 2 to 3 times a week to improve your condition. I also recommend 2 workshops, Initial Awakening & Finding True Self. They are on the weekends and are 1 full day and 2 full days. This is the best way to get started for you.

I had no idea how involved this would be. "I'm used to going to class once a week. I have my husband, family, and work. I spend time with my husband and family on the weekends. My husband will be interested too. I want to talk to him about it before I decide anything more. I can't spend any more money before talking to him about it. We used to belong to a spiritual study together."

She advised me, "This is for you; I suggest focusing on yourself. He can join if he wants after you get started."

"I understand, but for now I'll do the 10 classes to start."

"Ok, you can upgrade after a couple of weeks to an unlimited membership with a workshop if you want. I'll check in with you after a week or so."

After leaving I realized how much I needed this. I was grateful to feel so welcomed there.

My body was suffering along with my mind. I was having extreme digestive issues, losing sleep, losing weight, getting medical tests, and desperately taking medications and supplements to resolve my discomfort. My mind was always racing and feeling like there was something more I should do or say to others or shouldn't have said to others. My body was very painful, which was shadowing my thoughts and overactive mind activity. I was getting Botox injections for Dystonia, but I still had stiffness and tension in my upper body and neck.

I had watched Eckhart Tolle and Oprah's Live Webinar. He was saying all the right things, but I couldn't apply what he was saying in my life. I read a few of his books, and it wasn't working for me. I was still searching desperately for peace in my mind and body.

Prescription medications for acid reflux, irritable bladder, blood pressure, and muscle relaxants for Cervical dystonia crowded my kitchen counter. I was also still going for Botox injections quarterly for Cervical Dystonia. Diagnosed with irritable bowel also, I tried managing all of it on my own, but something had to change. I was only 52 years old.

Tapping My Abdomen

♥

When the student is ready the teacher appears.

I came in the door, put my shoes on the rack and silenced my phone, putting my purse in the back of the training room. I was there for my first class. The walls and floor were golden yellow, padding underneath the floor made the floor soft and cushiony. Cheerful music filled the room along with the sweet smell of palo santo.

Men and women, both younger and older than me, were standing in a circle tapping their abdomens. I wasn't sure what this abdomen tapping was about, but I did it because everyone was doing it. Everyone took turns counting to 10 as we progressed to 100, 200, and 300.

Deanna, the teacher, was a young woman with wavy long black hair. Mya, whom I felt so connected to and comforted me at my introductory session, wasn't there. Deanna seemed friendly, but not as warm as Mya.

After we stopped the belly tapping, we lined up into three rows facing the teacher, who stood in front, and the class began.

"Bangapsamnida" she greeted us, bowing as everyone did the same to her and each other. Body & Brain comes from South Korea. This greeting means "Hello beautiful being from heaven."

Behind the teacher was a large banner with a deep blue background and other colors, like a rainbow that formed a circle. On the side of this large banner were plants and a table where the music was set up.

After stretching, rotating our neck, shoulders, hips, knees, and ankles, we did an exercise called "Plate Balancing." This movement was a little confusing at first, moving our arms in different directions, but it felt amazing for my shoulders and chest.

Most of the movements were simple but felt foreign to me compared to the yoga I had practiced for 10 years.

Next it was time to lay down on the padded floor. Now I could relax my loosening, tired body.

A tribal, rhythmic beat began to vibrate through the room.

"Straighten your legs and tap your toes. Tap your toes, twisting your legs, breathing out." My thighs began to burn quickly, and I wanted to stop. This motion was challenging for my body and mind. We did this toe tapping for 5 minutes until the teacher instructed us to slowly stop.

A peaceful song, birds singing and water flowing streamed into my being next. Tears began to fill my eyes and drip onto my cheeks. My mind was quiet, and my body finally relaxed. The tension in my mind and body released into the floor, breathing deeply. Not aware of why I cried, but it felt as if a dam was releasing, and I had no choice but to let it open.

"Put your hands on your lower abdomen and breathe. Inhale as you expand your belly like a balloon. Exhale as you contract your belly." Breathing was always challenging for me. I got confused about which time I should expand and contract. I didn't care; I just felt at peace.

"Stretch your body. Arms up and point your toes. Bring your arms down and rub your hands together above your chest. Massage your face and sweep down your arms, squeeze your neck, sweep down your body. Slowly turn to the side and sit up. Rub your hands together, and clap 20 times. Now separate your hands a couple of inches apart. Notice if you feel any sensations between your hands. Move your hands away and together slowly feeling the energy gathering in your hands. The energy you feel we call Life Particles. It's healing particles of the Universe. Everything is made of Life Particles."

I followed the instructions but didn't feel any sensations. This was a mystery.

After class, everyone got up from the floor and moved to the back of the room. Deanna poured tea into small ceramic cups with no handles. The tea smelled heavenly and tasted like cinnamon and comfort.

Deanna asked us how we felt, going around the circle one by one. One woman shared, "I feel warm, relaxed, and I felt a lot of energy flowing in my body today." Another shared, "I came into class very tense; it was a hard day at work, and now I feel peaceful." When it was my turn, I shared, "I feel relaxed and peaceful. I began to cry when we were laying down. I'm not sure why." She assured us anything is okay, that we should just be aware of our thoughts and feelings.

When Deanna left the room, a few of us stayed and enjoyed our tea. I felt like I wanted to stay there as long as I could. My mind and body were relaxed, and I felt comfortable with these people who had the same goals for peace as me. Class helped me to feel at peace in mind and body. I wasn't even embarrassed that I cried. I felt like anything was okay.

I floated home in my car, relaxed and peaceful after class. I started to clean the kitchen and put stuff away that had been on the counter for a while.

"Hey, there's a new episode of Modern Family that we recorded. Do you want to watch it?" Randy asked.

"I think I'm gonna clean the kitchen and put some stuff away. I'm tired of looking at all of it. You can watch one of your shows."

Prior to this, I would get home from work, cook dinner, eat, and watch TV most nights, falling asleep in the comfy chair and then going to bed by 9.

The next day at work, I wasn't yawning and lethargic like before. "I love my new yoga classes. I feel great," I would share with my coworkers. "Diane, maybe you can come try a class with me sometime."

I hung up the calendar on my file cabinet at work and circled the classes I planned on going to.

I began to attend classes 3 to 4 times per week, feeling so good and having fun. I scheduled any plans or appointments around class because I felt the need to keep going.

At the end of class, I was beginning to feel "energy" between my hands during the meditation. This sensation was tingly and vibrating, expanding between my hands and showering over my body, The room was filled with peace and harmony. I could feel it now. Also, more tears flowed at the end of class, and my whole being became lighter, resting more comfortably at night than I could ever remember.

Solar Body Challenge

♥

W hen Ilchi Lee was in the process of writing the book *The So-lar Body: The Secret to Natural Healing*, Body & Brain Mt. Prospect Center had a 30-day study where members would do three simple exercises for 10 minutes each and every day.

I volunteered to be part of the study. We needed to keep a daily journal of any changes we experienced during this time.

The three exercises were Dahnjon Tapping, Plate Balancing, and Toe Tapping.

The Dahnjon Tapping exercise is one of the unusual exercises for a newcomer but the most beneficial for quieting the mind and improving digestion, which was important to me. The lower Dahnjon is two inches below the navel is the center of the physical body and energy body. We want to gather energy there and focus on grounding and centering our energy too. There are three Dahnjons, one in the lower abdomen for the physical body energy, one in the chest for the emotional or energy body, and one in the head for the spiritual body.

Plate Balancing is a great motion that involves moving the arms in a circular motion to open all the joints in the body and also the chest and shoulders deeply. This exercise has always been a favorite of mine. This was another area that I needed healing in, since I carried so much stress and tension there.

Toe Tapping helps quiet the mind and is used for insomnia. It helps you to fall asleep by tapping the feet together and breathing out, using the energy built up from the stress of the day. It also helps to loosen hips and thighs too.

I noticed many benefits from these exercises. It was a new beginning of self-care for me.

A few of my journal entries for the *Solar Body* Challenge:

Day 1 – 9/24/14

Neck and upper body pain and stiffness, stomach upset

After Dahnjon Tapping, felt better

Right shoulder popping while doing plate balancing

Felt invigorated, energetic after. Right side sore.

Right side weak

* Decided to stop taking muscle relaxant before bed to see how my condition improves!

Day 15 – 10/11/14

Saturday morning. It's time to clean house but first I did Dahnjon Tapping and Plate Balancing. It's so nice to be with myself and I feel at peace. I'm getting stronger; noticing my tendencies and habits. Feeling energy and my hands as I write. I can get through my darkness; it's all part of the process. I am graceful and have strength from within. Bowels are easier to move this morning.

I had a great day, more energy than expected after the long day yesterday. I'm amazed.

Day 18 – 10/14

I felt stiff in the morning. I did Dahnjon Tapping and Plate Balancing. Feeling better. I felt positive and physically better today. Feeling good about my practice and healing.

My neck is loosening up, turning to the right becoming easier.

Day 22 – 10/18

Neck moving better; able to balance muscles to hold it up better every day. I felt a lot of energy today during class. My heart is opening; chest feels lighter. I feel loneliness fading.

* 3 weeks no Klonopin, (muscle relaxant) no Botox shots for 4 months. I'm so happy to be free of these poisons in my body. I can heal myself!

Randy and the kids were starting to notice the change in my condition. I was a bit nervous about not going for Botox injections, but wanted to try. I didn't like relying on them every few months and wanted to try something else. I kept the Klonopin just in case, but I didn't take it anymore.

"Mom, you look great. Yoga is good for you. I'm so happy you're feeling better." Teresa knew how much I suffered.

Day 29 – 10/23

It was hard getting up early today, but I did it. I was going to just do Plate Balancing because of class later, but felt I had to do both. I called energy to my palms and felt it immediately. It was a very nice time. I felt peaceful and loving to myself. I hugged myself and realized my strength and determination. I feel warm and grateful.

10/24/14

Solar Body Challenge ends. I stayed consistent with the exercises and noticed a change in bowel movements and neck and shoulder stiffness. Also, my inner confidence and self-love is growing. I am grateful to be part of this challenge. I now have tools for life to help my body and mind condition. I will continue the exercises to keep improving my health.

After this experience, I began to realize that contrary to the Christian Science belief, our body is the reflection of our mind and spirit. When our mind and spirit aren't healthy, our body suffers.

Going Deeper: Guilt & Shame from Past

I began to read books by Ilchi Lee. The first book I read was *Life Particle Meditation: A Practical Guide to Healing and Transformation*.

I wasn't much of a reader at the time, but I read this book as if I was thirsty for what I needed to learn from it. It was about energy and how it affects our lives from a scientific approach. It gave examples such as plants that were spoken to lovingly were much healthier than plants ignored and spoken to negatively. This is an idea I heard about before, but this time, the thought went deeper.

I learned that I had a lot of negative talk, which was coming from me. I judged and blamed myself a lot. It was time to change this and learn to love and accept myself.

I longed to be loved and accepted. I had a sexual encounter while in junior high school and regret not having the respect and value for myself to say no.

In 7th grade I had a crush on Patrick. He had red hair and freckles, which I thought at the time was cute. He teased me by calling me names like "Nose Ann." He pulled my bra strap and boyish stuff like that. Since he paid attention to me, I thought he liked me.

I had my friend ask if he liked me, and he told her to "Have her meet me alone, behind the building by the tree after school."

I went out the door and saw him sitting by the tree. He didn't say anything to me, but sat down on the grass and motioned for me to sit beside him.

He began to rub his hands all over my body and pulled my pants and underpants down as he started to get on top of me. It all happened so quickly, and before I knew it, I felt his thing inside me. It was abrupt and painful. I wanted to scream. He got up from the ground and closed his pants, starting to leave.

Stupidly, I thought he liked me. I asked him, "Aren't you going to kiss me?" He had finished his mission. This was clear.

I collected myself, pulling my pants up in tears and shock. I felt used, stupid, and alone.

I was so ashamed that I allowed this to happen. I carried shame and guilt for many years until I could forgive myself for allowing this to happen. I was only looking for someone to love me.

I wasn't taught about self-respect or love. Nobody told me I was special or beautiful.

I remember my close friend, Karen, praising me, telling me, "You are pretty" when I was 13 years old.

I was shocked, answering, "Really, do you think so?"

My self-esteem was low because nobody taught me that I was valuable and precious. Just like the plants in the *Life Particle Meditation* book, I couldn't thrive as a young girl without praise and attention.

11/7/2014

Today I had my first private session:

It was such a powerful experience it scares me. I was overtaken by energy. I felt so much pain, my chest, my leg, it scared me. I couldn't sleep after the session. I was still so wired. I thought I could go insane. My heart pounded all night. Randy was mad about me being late, so it made things worse. I don't want to lose what I have. I just want to change how I feel and react to things. Is that possible? Is that selfish? I have a lot of wounds in my past to heal. I must love and accept them all one by one. I've made many mistakes in my life because I was so lonely and scared.

I looked to everyone else, everywhere else to be loved. Nobody else can fill my empty heart.

Before class, I felt like the teachers had been arguing. I could feel the energy of discord between them. I guess they are human and have emotions, after all. We are all the same. If we have a body, we have desires. I feel so much love from each of them, not sure how to handle how I felt today. I was uneasy. I didn't expect to feel that way. I will go back and just continue for my own healing. It doesn't matter what else goes on between them. It's not about me, but sometimes I feel it is.

I keep feeling the need to slow down. It's going so fast. I need time to let it all settle in. I am in charge of myself, and I will do what's best for me. Thank you to the universe for showing me the way to heal my heart. I am grateful for this opportunity.

11/8

Felt sick & tired all day after healing session.

11/9

Starting to feel more centered, still sick, and tired.

Resistance to change coming up in my mind. I don't want to let go of my comfortable life, of living for social activities and material gain. It's not always so comfortable anyway but, change is hard.

Randy is getting mad about me spending so much time at the center. I don't like that he's mad at me. I wish he could understand. He doesn't know what's going on, really. He only knows what I'm telling him. It's so different from our past spiritual study in Japan. I feel so much more this time than before. I hope he can join me soon to experience the difference for himself.

My lonely heart searched for love my whole life. I am so lucky to have found someone to love me for who I am. Thank you Randy for loving me for my heart also and encouraging me to find my soul. We are one in spirit.

Bird of the Soul

T he Book, *Bird of the Soul,* by Ilchi Lee touched my heart deeply from when I first read it. Waiting for an appointment at the center one time, I picked up the pink, colorful book from the shelf display. A large, playfully drawn white bird was on the cover and a young boy. The story was about a boy growing up, and as he grew, life became more difficult. He got married and had more responsibilities and worries. He lost his *Soul Bird,* since he was so busy with everything else that he had to take care of now. I wept as I read the book in the lobby. I was buried in responsibility and worry. This was my story and so true for most people. We forget about our dreams and hopes, and the freedom to be ourselves. All the dreams get buried under the burdens of growing up and being responsible.

I purchased the book, which included a meditation CD.

Sitting in my room on my pink yoga mat, lavender incense burning on my bedside table, I played the CD.

A man speaking in a gentle but strong voice guided, "Put your hands on your heart, and feel what emotion you are carrying." Background music brought up the feeling of sadness and loneliness.

"Feel this emotion and try to remember where this emotion came from."

A huge realization was awakened in my mind. The emotions of sadness and loneliness start from me. I have been and am the one in charge of my feelings, always.

"Now it's time to change the emotion and set yourself free." He guided next, "Open your arms, and start to move your wings to become free from these emotions." The kind, caring voice guided me to fly high and feel the freedom in my wings, soaring over the mountains and water. I would come to a place and rest on a mountaintop high above the water.

Huuuuh, I feel so freeee....... My chest feels lighter and more open.

As the meditation continued, I could see the sun starting to rise in the distance. I felt total freedom and serenity, picturing myself above the earth, sun rising in the distance. The music flowed and changed into this feeling of freedom and peace. Now I could begin to go back over the water and mountains, feeling the freedom in my wings. I was going back home with this newfound freedom.

I feel so peaceful and free. It all comes from me. This revelation radiated through my existence.

I purchased this book for each of my children, feeling so touched, and how important the message was to share. I don't know if anyone understood it as deeply as I felt it, but I wanted to make sure I gave them the opportunity.

Weekends were Randy's and my "together time." Sometimes we had different ideas of what that time would include. When I didn't agree with his sexual desires, it seemed that he would choose to go running with our daughter. I felt abandoned when he did this, feeling I should have gone along with his wishes so he would stay with me.

One Saturday, after doing this *Bird of the Soul* meditation when Randy was out running with Teresa, he came home, and I was weeping. "I feel so sad about myself and how my focus has been on materials and what other people want and think. I lost myself and my priorities. It's time for change." I cried most of the day as if I was shedding the burdens and worries that covered my heart. I believe my heart opened that day, and I found myself. *My Soul Bird,* my freedom to be me.

"Okay, honey, let me know if you need anything," Randy replied. I'm sure he had no idea what was going on, but he would go along.

As I wept, I realized how much I needed to change and how I would need to give up my old ways. I needed to stop focusing on what others needed, like physical affection or intimacy. I needed to draw boundaries when I wasn't interested or going somewhere. Sometimes, I wasn't up to going with friends or even family. I wept all day with sadness. I knew it was time to be true to myself now.

I realized what might be at risk when I made these changes. My relationships, including my marriage, were going to need to change, and I wasn't sure how everything would turn out in the end. I knew it was something I had to do, and I had to accept the risk.

Randy began to feel threatened by my newfound strength and being at classes all the time. "Why do you have to go to class every night.?" He would question. "We never see each other anymore."

"I'm sorry. I need to choose myself now. The classes are helping me feel so much better. We'll spend time on the weekend. I love you."

Initial Awakening-First Workshop

September 2014

After two months of going for class regularly, Deanna suggested I go for a workshop called Initial Awakening. This workshop would help me to learn more about energy and how to manage my energy and stay centered in my daily life. I upgraded my membership to 3 months, and this workshop would be included.

Initial Awakening was on a Sunday from 9am to 5pm. Randy seemed a little frustrated when I told him about the amount of time it was. I had hesitated for a month after she suggested it initially, but now I was curious. I didn't like to spend that much time away from home, but maybe it was necessary. I was beginning to trust Deanna.

Upon arriving the day of the workshop, there were people I didn't know helping to check us in. I was given a label with my name on it once I signed in.

Four rows of chairs were set up and a white board was in front of the training room where class usually was and a small table and chair where the teacher would be. Several people from our center and other centers were there to participate.

We all gathered in a circle behind the chairs to exercise before the workshop would begin. Geum Dawoon the instructor for the day, wasn't in the room yet. After twenty minutes or so, they instructed us to have a seat. Geum Dawoon came out shortly after, and we greeted her with a standing bow and "Bangapsamnida," which means "Hello beautiful being" in Korean.

She wore a light blue loose fitting neatly ironed button up top and pants with white comfy slippers and socks. There was a comfortable brown leather chair for her to sit in as well.

"Bangapsamnida," she greeted us with a bright smile and a half bow.

Next, she asked each of us, "What is your name, which center do you go to, and what do you hope to get from the workshop?"

Some people answered that they wanted to learn how to stay centered in their life, that sometimes they feel life is out of control. Others said that they do so much for everyone else and don't have time or energy for themselves and that they feel like something is missing.

I answered, "I want to become emotionally stronger and more confident in myself."

She drew a picture of a cup of water representing energy on the whiteboard. She explained how we give our time and energy by doing for others like our parents, children, spouse, and coworkers, and the cup becomes empty. We need to refill our cup, so we have something to give; otherwise, there's nothing left to give. Refilling our cup of energy could be many things, such as exercise, meditation, breathing, and resting.

Another part of the workshop was an experiment with negative and positive feedback and noticing the difference in these energies. We paired up and while having one arm raised at chest level, our partner would try to push it down while speaking. "You are amazing, so smart, and such a good person." Next, our partner would say, "You're stupid, lazy, and you'll never succeed" while trying to push the arm down. The strength of the arm was better, of course, with the positive voices and weak with the negative voices.

This was quite interesting to me and brought up many thoughts about my life until then. I always blamed and judged myself, never feeling good enough. I tried to be a good friend to everyone and a good listener, to be a good person, although it was exhausting. I didn't love myself, that I knew.

At one moment, I was overwhelmed with gratitude for finally finding some answers for myself and how to strengthen my low self-esteem. I searched for a learning ground like this my whole life.

We also did exercises that were challenging for me. I was weak at the time and stiff. Exercises like "Sleeping Tiger" really challenged my limitations. We would hold our arms and legs up in the air while lying on our backs, focusing on relaxation and breathing. Many times, I spoke to myself, "I am strong, I can do it," while my legs shook like crazy. When we finally put our arms and legs down, the sense of accomplishment was powerful.

When we sat up and did the hands opening and closing meditation, I felt the "Life Particles." It was powerful to feel the tingling and vibrating sensations of energy between my hands. My brain was shut off and my arms flowed through the air expressing peace from heaven, which I felt deeply in my mind and body.

I learned exercises to gather energy and calm down my emotions, too. They were simple exercises I could do during my daily life such as Dahnjon Tapping, intestine exercises, and breathing. –See Self-Healing Resources section for exercises from the *Solar Body* Book by Ilchi Lee.

After the workshop, I felt happy. I had spent the day learning important things, and my body and mind felt strong and light. Also, I wasn't worried about what was going on at home, what I may be missing all day, because I was interested in what I was learning. This was all a triumph for me.

Randy was starting to get used to being on his own more, getting stuff done around the house and having time to himself. We were growing individually, and our relationship was evolving, too.

Finding True Self Workshop

♥

October 2014

You've always had wings you just needed to find the courage to fly.

Finding True Self was the next workshop that Deanna suggested I attend. This workshop would help balance the heart chakra. I was nervous about this one for a few different reasons. It was all weekend long, from 9 am to 7pm Saturday and Sunday. The location was the Northbrook center so I would need to drive myself there and home which was about 20 minutes away. I also wouldn't be home for the whole weekend. I would miss spending time with my husband, and he might see our kids without me. This was a big decision.

Randy drove me to Northbrook for a preparation training Thursday night before the workshop. He dropped me off, went home, and came to pick me up a couple hours later. He was always supportive of me and this time he went out of his way.

Twenty minutes after it was supposed to be finished, I got to the car. He asked with curiosity and frustration "What's going on, you're pretty late. Is everything ok?"

"Yes, sorry. The class went a little longer."

"What did you do tonight?"

"We did some exercises and talked about what we want to get from the workshop and some other games to prepare for the workshop. I'm not supposed to talk about it, sorry. I'm a little bit nervous, but I think it's gonna be good for me."

"Okay, I guess you know what you're doing. It's gonna be a long weekend. Can you drive here on your own?"

"Yes, I'll be fine. Thanks for taking me tonight. Thanks for always supporting me in whatever I do. I think I need to do this for myself. I hope you understand."

"Okay. Whatever you need to do, I'm behind you."

"I love you so much."

"I love you too."

I didn't sleep much the night before the workshop. I was nervous about being away for two days from my husband and life. I was nervous about driving myself to a place I wasn't familiar with 20 minutes from home, and I had no idea what we would be doing at the workshop.

I asked the teachers what we would be doing, but nobody could tell me about the workshop. "That would be like spoiling a movie telling you the ending" Deanna answered. I looked up the workshop online to see if I could find anything out but found nothing. The anticipation and mystery made me anxious.

I got to the workshop, and there were 18 people attending. There were chairs set up in the training room like the previous workshop. The room was bright yellow with the golden padded floor like the other center and the Blue Banner in the front of the room.

Happy music playing, as we began our day in a circle exercising, just like regular class.

Since this workshop is Body & Brain exclusive; I can't share the contents. The activities, lecture, and exercise brought up memories, emotions. There were several teachers there from other centers who helped through the workshop. After the first day, I felt emotionally and physically drained, but hopeful.

At the end of the day, we were advised to go home and rest. "Stay focused on yourselves and try not to talk to others at home a lot or on the phone. We suggest you don't watch television or engage in social media either. This will help you get the most from the weekend workshop."

Driving myself home that night by myself, in the dark, I had lots to reflect on about the day. I felt accomplished making it through the long day and being independent to drive myself home.

Randy was excited to hear about my day. "How did everything go? What did you do?"

"I'm sorry, honey. I can't talk much. Everything went fine. I need to eat and rest. I have another long day tomorrow. I'm exhausted. I also have homework to do," I explained.

He sighed with frustration. He was clearly not happy with my answer. We weren't used to spending so much time apart, and he was upset to hear I couldn't share about what went on at the workshop.

I felt bad, but I had begun this journey and wanted to do my best to stay focused and get the benefit from the workshop. I was emotionally drained and exhausted. We also had a writing assignment to do for the next day. I was looking forward to doing the work and was comfortable staying focused inside. It took about thirty minutes. I fell asleep quickly after I finished.

The next day, we went deeper emotionally through exercises and activities. More tears were shed, lots of sweating, and challenging exercises, too.

This weekend was a journey to find my True Self, my true essence. I was able to open my heart and accept myself and other key people in my life.

This workshop is one I recommend everyone to experience in their lives to heal the past and open themselves to who they are. I am Free to Be Me!

Finding True Self changed how I view myself. I found freedom to be me. I also realized I have the strength to push through challenges that have come up and will come up. I realized how valuable I am as a human being.

I found a new way of looking at relationships with people close to me and experiences from my past, helping to heal painful memories that I was holding on to. This workshop changed my life.

In the past, I worried about what other people thought of me. I was concerned about saying the right thing and doing the right thing and always questioned myself. After the workshop, I became confident about my choices and actions. I acknowledged my strengths and weaknesses.

I dance when I hear music that I enjoy now. When a song comes on the radio that I know, I sing along. I am comfortable in my own skin. I am the same person, but I feel good about who I am. I'm not perfect by any means, but I'm me, and that is enough. I depend on my own opinion now instead of always asking others. I enjoy spending time with myself because I have me and that's all I need.

After this weekend, I became a different person. People were noticing the changes in me.

My daughter Teresa said, "You seem more relaxed than before. I'm so happy you found something for yourself. I think it's great for you."

Randy admitted, "Whatever went on at that workshop seems to have helped you. I'm happy you are feeling better about yourself. It seems like you feel better physically, too."

My daughter-in-law, Ashley, said I seemed happier and more positive.

I was thrilled to get this positive feedback from my family. These words confirmed how I was feeling. I felt like a new person.

Journal entry after finding true self:

I feel like I'm going on a journey to a place deep inside. I've been there before. A journey to connect once again to my true self. I remember the warmth inside that I am. I want to go back.

This world of the 5 senses can make me feel so uneasy. There are so many expectations from others that I am concerned about. I got lost in all the people pleasing. It all makes me feel so vulnerable.

I am looking for peace.

Will people understand what I'm going through? Will they stand beside me or walk away?

I can't do what's expected of me anymore. I want to follow my heart, but I am afraid I will lose my comfort and security. The thought makes me feel lonely.

I am so dependent on others' approval and support. That is who I was. I will no longer be that person. I have peace inside myself. I have me. That's all I need. I don't need anyone else to approve of me. My heart is full of love.

Ups and downs are part of growth!

11/5/14

What happened? I see everything clearly, but I want to go back to the way it was. I'm not sure if I can go back. In some ways it was more comfortable there, just going along and not stirring up feelings of insecurity and hurt.

I have felt so much change these past couple of months, not sure what is happening. I am not ready to face more of the emotional pain of my past that I'm carrying inside. I'm not sure I have the strength to do this. I'm afraid of what might happen. I don't want to lose anything that I have now. I feel different. I don't care about new clothes and material things I did before. I don't feel the same about my life and the priorities I had before like socializing. I guess I just need to trust and keep going. I've been searching my whole life for direction & purpose. I finally found it. I want to live as my true self and help others do the same. I can't turn away.

Each of us has our own darkness to face. We are all the same. It doesn't go away because we are enlightened. It keeps showing up looking for the light.

I am here. Look at me. I am the best. Please love me, accept me. I am the best.

I have searched for love my whole life outside of myself. My body was something I could give for love in return. I was born with a lonely heart.

I thought boys/men would like me if I did what they wanted. I am so ashamed. I did many things because I felt lonely.

Growth isn't always uphill:

10/29

Will I ever be able to forgive my mistakes? I have made many. I was a sad and lonely child, always looking for love outside of myself. I didn't know any better. I always thought I had to give myself to others to be loved. I always felt I wouldn't be good enough. I tried to do a good job and get good grades in school, and my parents would say, "Why didn't you do this?" They couldn't say the words I wanted to hear. I am angry at how they treated me. I was lonely and afraid. I tried hard to be good to be recognized but could never feel proud of myself. I always sought attention from boys to make me feel better. I craved affection and attention from men as I grew. I would give anything to be accepted and loved.

11/18

I am true self. I have guilt and shame about my past. I'm tired of holding my bad decisions from when I was young and promiscuous. I have punished myself enough. I have a heavy heart because I can't accept the choices I made. I suffered my whole life with guilt. I was so afraid, and now I'm so painful.

These are mistakes made by the human, JoAnn. That is not my true self.

It's okay. JoAnn, remember I was with you then. I was with you, loving you, accepting your choices. It's what you had to do at those times. You learned from those mistakes, and you moved on. You have a warm open heart accepting others. Why can't you love and accept yourself? You are not perfect. You have a body to see these errors of your heart. Now it's time to move forward. Love and accept yourself as you are. The past is done, and all is okay now. I am with you always. Remember me. I am your true self. I'm loving you always. I've been waiting for you to notice me.

Is this all a dream? Some of it makes sense more than others. I believe what I am feeling, but what am I feeling? Am I just going through the motions? I have such doubt. I have changed inside, and I feel stronger, but I feel worn down by Randy. He seems to go along, then he backs off. It's been so frustrating. Is it all for money? I have felt such energy and love but also resistance. Is this a test of my strength? I feel weak and tired. Why do I need approval from anyone else? It has been good for me. I feel stronger and not so affected by others' emotions, but still, I feel weak.

One week ago, I was on the path to finding my true self. I found it and bounced right back to my old ways. My anger and frustration took over, and I was so angry I couldn't contain myself.

My family (siblings and parents) is such a mess. What can I do? Send healing energy every day, that's all. My mind is so occupied with money. Am I still covering up my true self? It's so hard to let go and trust. Certain things need to be done to live in this world.

It's all about balance. Thanks for loving and accepting me as I am. My soul, I love you, and I am here with you always.

12/13

I am still afraid to be alone. What would I do if he leaves me? I want to be free to be me, unattached to anyone else and their choices. I am my own person. My heart is being stifled. I'm afraid to be me because he doesn't like it. I feel like I'm being dragged down by his desires. This life I've lived so far isn't what my heart wants. I must create what I want.

12/23

I have so much anger and blame toward others. I thought I was loving, but I didn't notice these emotions I have. My true self is love and acceptance, unconditional. The layers of emotion and preconceptions are covering who I really am. Who am I? How can I help anyone when I have anger and blame? I don't like anyone that doesn't recognize me as wonderful. I feel so heavy and unhappy today. What have I been doing all this time? Am I fooling myself? Is that all an illusion?

I want to live as my true self. Will I ever get there? I get so discouraged.

12/25

I'm learning this is my body but is not it's not me, meaning my body is a vehicle for my soul. My soul is the real me.

Marriage Changing

♥

Love is like a butterfly—undergoing metamorphosis to achieve its most exquisite self.

M y life began to change, along with my close relationships, and I began to feel more self-assured and healthier in my body and mind.

I was no longer feeling the need to please others to be loved. I was comfortable to say no if I wasn't interested in doing something when asked. Previously I would do things to please others even when my heart wasn't in it.

A new life began for me now, being who I wanted to be, not who others wanted me to be or thought I should be.

My close friend that I talked to about most everything began to wonder about our relationship.

She would text me, "Are you mad at me? You don't reach out lately. Is everything ok?"

"Yes, I'm fine. I'm not upset with you. I'm just enjoying yoga classes more now. We will talk soon."

I was learning to count on myself instead of reaching out to her or anyone else for reassurance. She was concerned about me at the time, thinking I was getting into something that may not be healthy. "I'm worried about you. This seems to be taking a lot of your time."

"Classes are great. I'm feeling so much better. You should come try a class. The teachers and people are so nice."

I was not so dependent on Randy's opinions or ideas about things. He noticed these changes and wasn't always happy about them.

"Have you noticed that I'm not complaining anymore about being sick? I love the exercises and the people, plus I'm feeling so much better. You should come with me." I pleaded.

"You're right, sorry. I'm happy for you. Maybe next week. There's a game on tonight, anyway." He answered.

Being true Soul Mates means allowing each other to grow individually, without attachment.

7/20 Soul mate reflection:

I found someone who needed me as much as I needed them, and we clung to each other, satisfying each other's needs and raising a beautiful family. We expanded ourselves but never really knew the purpose of our lives, so our family was just as confused as us. Each of us has a different gift, but we cover those gifts until we awaken to our true selves and purpose. We feel so much and connect to what is real, but when we hit an uncomfortable part in our journey, we leave because it doesn't suit us anymore. This has been our life until now.

I am finding my strength, value, and my independence now. I've stopped feeling the need to please others, realizing I was selling my soul for comfort and attachment all along. I have my own value and worth separate from anyone else and what they can do for me. I have me. I have my own divinity and connection to mother earth, and I don't need any other physical attachment to anyone to be one with me, my true self.

I am free to be me despite what anyone thinks of me or can do for me. I am me. That's all that matters. I have my own value individual of any other person or what I physically do for anyone else. I choose me and my freedom to be me.

I will not make myself small for anyone else anymore. I have infinite value. I am creative. I am warm. I am giving. I am love. I can create what I want without anyone's opinion. I am one with my soul. I am free and healthy. I give energy and healing to others around me. I am heaven and earth in my body. I am expansive, no more boundaries.

Metamorphosis

♥

I only ask to be free. Butterflies are free. –by Charles Dickens

After attending classes for a couple months regularly and participating in workshops I was starting to feel better physically also. I was taking less supplements for my digestion and feeling more able to control my emotions. My digestion improved and my body felt less tense. I had found hope and peace for myself finally at 52 years old.

I had a doctor visit about six months after starting classes. "JoAnn, what are you doing for yourself? You look great?" my doctor inquired when she saw me.

"I started taking yoga classes at Body & Brain. I feel so much better."

"Let's go over your meds now to update what you're taking. Are you still taking, Klonopin?"

"No." I answered.

"How about Prevacid?"

"No."

"Detrol?"

"No."

"Lisiniprol for blood pressure?"

"Yes"

"Your blood pressure is good today. Let's see if we can get you off that one too. Don't take it for a week and monitor your blood pressure every day. If it's ok for a week, you can stop. It's a low dose so it should be ok. I'm amazed at the changes you've made. Keep doing what you're doing!"

"Thank you doctor, I will. I love the classes."

I started to realize why I had so many health issues. My body was reflecting everything that was going on with my energy and state of mind. I was worrying about what others thought and expected of me and having so much stress and guilt about my actions and words. I would always wonder after having a conversation with people in my life if I said the right thing or hurt someone's feelings. I felt self-conscious most of the time. Through these classes and workshops, I began to realize how I was wasting my energy in so many ways. If I continued with my self-sabotaging thoughts and worries, I would continue to be sick. I had to keep going and continuing to change and get stronger physically and emotionally through this journey I started.

This was unbelievable when I realized how much healthier I had gotten through moving my body and releasing the stress that I carried for many years. I had to keep going!

Across the Hall

♥

My daughter's room was empty, with a twin bed across the hall from our room, and Randy was a loud snorer. I began spending more time there, doing reflection before bed and having space for myself.

Randy started to feel abandoned. I loved him as always, but I needed to do this for myself.

"What's going on? Don't you love me anymore?" he asked.

"I'm sorry, honey. Of course, I love you. I just need some time for myself at night. I'm doing a lot of journaling and reflection. I can lay with you for a while if you want to talk. I'll show you toe tapping. It helps you sleep better." As the bed vibrated with our toes tapping, we talked about our day and fell asleep. I would wake up from his snoring and go to the room across the hall and journal before going back to sleep.

Our relationship was evolving, and he wasn't happy about it. I was more independent, not looking to him for approval or security as much as before.

Before I needed to have him agree with me by the end of a discussion, but now, I would accept that we had our own opinions. I was an individual now with my own opinions about life.

He had to get used to the idea that I wasn't the co-dependent wife I had once been.

"I'm not sure if I like the way things are now," he would confess.

My heart would sink when I heard these words. I had to be strong and trust in my heart that I was on the right path for my own healing and self. If he was ready for growth and change, he would accept our new relationship and the new me.

I asked myself now, what really changed? Who was I before?

I believe my confidence and trust in myself grew. I didn't back off about what I felt or believed was fair. I didn't trust myself before, and I would waiver when he disagreed with what I said or did. Now I trusted myself most.

Change can be challenging but, in our hearts, we knew it was necessary.

Randy Starting Body & Brain

After a few months, I finally convinced Randy to come for classes. He enjoyed the stretching and relaxation time, but when class was over, he was ready to leave. I would ask "Don't you want to stay for tea?"

He always made an excuse, "We should go. The dog has been home alone all day and we need to get dinner."

After this happened a few times, he would say.

"I'll go to class, but let's drive separately. Then you can stay as long as you want."

He liked some of the classes more than others. He didn't like the Vibration class. It made him feel uncomfortable with all the dancing and free movement. This class was on Friday evening so we would go to "Naf Naf" at Randhurst for dinner after or pick up pizza from Rosati's. I would usually let him choose where we would go to eat if he came for class with me.

I was thrilled that he was joining me now. What I hoped for was happening. Could we continue together?

Energy Principles Together

♥

E nergy Principles Workshop was being offered at one of the other centers and Deanna suggested we go to it together. I never knew how he would react to new situations, new people, and new experiences. His interest in classes wavered daily at this point.

The workshop was set up with chairs and yellow walls, a golden padded floor, and the Blue Life Particle Banner in the front of the room like at the other centers. Happy music played as we came in, and we were greeted warmly by the teachers who checked us in. We signed the waiver and received name tags to put on our shirts. There were people from other centers for the workshop too.

Forming a circle in the back of the room, we did some exercises together, guided by one of the teachers, before the workshop began. We took our seats, and the trainer, whose name was Younglim, came in. We greeted her with a "Bangapsamnida" and a half bow, and she greeted us back with the same respect. Sitting in our seats now, she introduced herself.

"I started Body & Brain 10 years ago. I was a Neurochemist for 20 years and was successful but not happy. My son became very ill, and I was searching for a way to manage the stress at this difficult time. Body & Brain has helped me physically and emotionally. I realized I needed to make a change for myself and my family. I decided to change my career, so I left neurochemistry and started working with the Body & Brain center in Libertyville. Now I'm helping others change their lives. I'm grateful to meet you all today and teach you about Energy Principles."

She then began explaining about how significant energy is in our daily life. We did some partner exercises, experiencing energy and how it works and feels. It was a powerful day, and Randy was interested in what was being said and the experience he was having.

The teacher had a humorous approach, and Randy respected her for her professional background. The workshop lasted 4 hours, and I tried my best to focus on myself and not him. My goal was to focus on me and what I was learning and feeling.

Once we got in the car to go eat, we started talking about the day. "I enjoyed the workshop today. I'm glad you convinced me to go. She was a great teacher. It was very interesting to learn about energy and how it works in our bodies and minds," he shared.

"I'm so glad you liked it. I learned a lot too. It's so amazing. I feel like I've looked for something like this my whole life."

He was starting to feel the benefits of classes and the workshop firsthand.

Everything was starting to come together, and our relationship was evolving into being soulmates on this new journey. I was so happy to have him by my side, yet I knew I had to keep focusing on myself.

Sometimes I didn't feel up to going to class. "Let's go. You'll feel better once you finish," he'd say.

"You're right; let's go." After class, "I feel so much better. Let's go to the store and pick up a few things."

I was amazed at my physical and emotional strength and how different I felt. We were helping each other grow in ways I could never have imagined. We had raised a family together and went through a lot of difficult times, but this was different. I felt a drive in my gut that I had never had before. I had to keep going.

This was more important than anything I had ever done in my life.

Valentine's Day Weekend 2015

♥

T his is a Valentine's Day I will always remember. Randy agreed to take Finding True Self! My old self would have never agreed for him to do something without me for this special weekend.

He experienced this life changing workshop for himself and woke up to his value and purpose.

After he finished the weekend, we could share about the workshop and different experiences throughout the weekend. This was a deep bonding experience for us. We spoke of our deepest awakenings and our lives up until then. We now walked the same path. My heart was happy. My soulmate was truly beside me now. I could be myself and we could grow together.

Our First Trip to Sedona Mago Center

April 2015

I learned of an opportunity to meet Ilchi Lee who was the founder of Body & Brain during a Solar Body Program at Sedona Mago Center in Arizona.

I remember someone teasing me, "You're going straight to the top meeting Ilchi Lee. I guess you don't mess around."

"Can we afford to go for this training? We have plenty of other things to spend money on." Randy said.

"I'd rather spend money on us instead of the house, at this point in my life," I argued.

"I guess you're right. Let's do it. Sedona is beautiful."

We were always seeking peace, sharing a spiritual interest, and now we found a path to follow.

Randy and I traveled to Sedona for the Solar Body program. We were excited about being able to meet Ilchi Lee during this program. We flew into Phoenix and rented an economy car to drive to Sedona. Hearing from others at the center about the bumpy road to get into the retreat center, we were curious.

Once we turned onto Bill Gray Road, we knew what everyone was talking about. The road was bumpy, dusty, and sandy orange, with open fields on either side and burnt orange mountains in the distance. After bouncing up and down for 20 minutes or so, we began to see some red hills and small buildings. Ilchi Road was at the end of the bumpy road, and a smiling gnome–like character with a thumb up gesture greeted us at the intersection. We finally arrived at Sedona Mago Center for Well–being and Retreat. The Welcome Center was just up the road. Getting out of the car, we noticed the peaceful silence.

The Welcome Center had a store with clothes that the Body & Brain instructors wore, posters we had seen at the yoga studios, crystals, and other interesting items.

We stood in line with others who were arriving for the event as well. An energy of excitement and a happy reunion filled the space. Many of the people seemed to know each other, exchanging hugs, sharing about where they were from, and asking us where we were from.

After signing in, we were given keys to our casita on a neck string to keep handy. We also received a map of the retreat center and dining hours. They pointed us in the direction of our casita and the dining hall and the hall where the event was taking place.

Charming red rock casitas filled in rows to the side and behind the welcome center.

All the buildings, including the dining hall, training hall, and casitas were spread out over 173 acres of land.

"Do you know where we're going?" I asked Randy. "I'll follow you."

"I think so. Let me take a look at the map. Okay, our room is 101, so it's down that way and up the steps."

The room had two beds and a red stone floor. There was a sink outside the bathroom with shelves on the side. Laying down on the comfy bed to rest after the long journey before dinner, we were excited to be there.

The dining hall was the next destination on our map. It was a few blocks from our casita, passing the beautiful red mountains in the distance and scented rosemary bushes and Juniper trees on our path. There was a metal turtle statue at the end of the road to the dining hall.

That made it easy to recognize the path next time, along with some signs directing us.

The food was served buffet-style with salads, fish, vegetables, and fruit. The menu was a pescatarian. It was all delicious. There were groups of people visiting and laughing like a family reunion. We joined a table and felt at ease right away. "Where are you from?" we were asked. "Have you been here before? How long have you been a member?"

After dinner, we joined a group of people going to the hall where the training was. We were greeted warmly and given name tags with our center on them, so everyone knew where we were from. Fun music came on, and everyone danced happily after travelling all day. The announcer told us about the event and gave us the schedule. They also announced the different states that everyone was from, and we cheered when Illinois was announced. There were about 100 people from all around the world for this program

As we walked out the door after the training, the night sky was dark with many stars lighting the sky. We carried flashlights to light our path, as recommended, but we had no idea how to get back to our room. As we wandered in the dark, trying to get our bearings, we saw someone else. "It's our first time here, and we can't figure out how to get back to our room."

"No problem. It gets dark here, and it's easy to get turned around. Room 101 is this way. I'll show you."

For a couple of days before meeting Ilchi Lee, we had training from other instructors. These instructors were the embodiment of joy, sincerity, and compassion. As they spoke, love radiated into the room of people and the exercises and music felt even more special than back home at the center.

The day arrived when he would come to the training hall to give us a lecture. Serious excitement filled the room of 100 people, anticipating his arrival. He came in waving to everyone and smiling from ear to ear, dressed comfortably in brightly colored, nicely pressed clothes and a top hat.

As he spoke in Korean, a young woman translated for us. I became sleepy, unable to comprehend most of what he said. I had been looking forward to meeting him and I couldn't keep my eyes open or focus.

As I looked around the room, others seemed to be struggling as well. I was disappointed but reassured by the instructors that this might happen since we weren't used to this pure energy.

Journal Entry 4/10/15:

Mago Garden is such a beautiful place, has wonderful food, includes very peaceful surroundings, and the energy is amazing. I find myself wanting to connect with others, but I feel like I'm not like them. I feel different. I'm feeling more warmth to others, slowly opening my heart. I felt lots of healing and love during the training. Walking in the healing garden was very special today. I felt one with nature. I felt the energy from the trees, water, and sun. The gentle breeze on my skin was soothing. I was very emotional, and it felt wonderful. I am a bright shining star in the universe, shining for everyone.

4/11

What a wonderful day. I woke up early to see the sunrise. It was cloudy but bright. I went to heaven and earth rock. There was a beautiful view all around. I asked for my mission, and I felt that I was meant to be here. I'm not sure what that means. We did meditation by the ancient Dahn Guhn statue. I could remember a past life that was a happy place, a paradise for everyone. We loved each other, and we were all happy together. I felt more connection with others today. We met Ilchi Lee tonight. He looked just like in the videos, but with such powerful energy as he spoke. We had lots of preparation before we could meet him. I kept imagining how he is the one that created Body & Brain Yoga Tai Chi and wrote all the books I have read. They mean so much to me and touch my heart. I had horrible stomach pain. My body was trying to release the stagnant energy. I had chills as well. It felt like I was being healed, letting go of stagnant energy. I need time to rest. I'm sad I must go home tomorrow.

4/12 Journal Entry Back to Civilization

It was such a great experience. I experienced lots of cleaning up and clearing stagnant energy. I am aware that I'm part of nature. I have memories in my brain of a more peaceful time. I was there. Everyone loved each other.

4/13

Back to the outside world, with my true self in the background. Will I change? Have I changed? Am I imagining things? I'm so excited about any interest from my family. Will they feel what I do from the books I've given them? Will anyone take a step to change? Why am I so concerned about others, anyway? Am I looking for approval? It's just nice to share with others. I have so many friends on Facebook and people in class now. I have gained such true friends that have this common spiritual interest.

I was carefree in this environment, just being me. I always felt lucky to have such a nice family waiting for me at home. We are blessed with our family. My family, including my dad and siblings, is another story. There is so much work there. I hope I can help change that. It's so painful to realize that everyone is separate and doesn't get along. It's all in the mind and energy. My health and outlook have changed. I know that's real. I felt so much and have been touched by so many things. It's normal to question myself and difficult to give up so much that we are conditioned to. We believe our brains and those thoughts take over our body and soul in this world. It's so hard to give up our habits and comforts. Randy is starting to feel benefits from the practice as well. I'm so happy he's joining me on this journey.

Life's Purpose

What do I want? What is the purpose of my life?

These were some of my deep awakenings from my spiritual journey so far.

Journal Entry 7/15

I want to help people realize who they are. Am I just the person in the mirror I see in the morning and the body that is covered in clothes? Am I the emotions that I feel when I'm upset or angry by what others say or do? Is there something else besides this body and false image I make up for others to see?

Since I was a girl, I remember feeling deeply about life and questioning why people did things. I was sad for myself and humanity. I was sad to see others tormented because of how they looked or what they did. We should all be free and loved for who we are, regardless of what others feel or think of us. We are our own person with individual talents and have the power to create happiness in different ways. We were all living together. We were one happy family, dancing and sharing our lives undivided. I remember such a time in a past life, but I don't know what happened.

We all have our pain and discomfort and look outside at others to find the answers. We are capable and responsible for how we feel and how we make others feel. It's the energy we share with those around us, and it spreads to all of humanity. We can change ourselves and others by realizing it's our responsibility. Materials are just fog over our true nature. Let's seek and find out how we can come back to who we really are. We each have our own key to health and happiness for ourselves, our community, and the earth. There are so many clouds in the way, so many attachments to the world around us. It's all a mistake.

We need food and shelter for our bodies to survive, but not the excess that we think we need. That's the separateness we've created from thinking our bodies and minds are who we really are. We need to remember this once again so we can live in harmony with the earth. Mother earth creates and sustains us from the air we breathe, the food we eat, and the water we drink. We take it all for granted because we don't know the truth about who we really are. This is my purpose: to awaken myself and share with others that we are one with Mother Earth.

I always thought others had it easier; they had a better situation, better parents, better friends, etc. I was born this lifetime to awaken to my true nature by the discomfort I experienced in this life. I always wanted something I didn't have. I thought if I had something different, I'd be happier. I heard happiness came from inside but never knew how to find it. I searched for acceptance from others my whole life, trying to attach myself to anyone who would have me. I was desperate. People would satisfy my needs for a while, but I always ended up alone and needing someone again. I never filled the void because I couldn't find it outside myself.

Solar Body Book Party

♥

After the *Solar Body* book was published in April 2015, we as practitioners of Body & Brain were on a mission to share the book. We felt that it could help everyone to manage their own wellbeing and live a happier, more harmonious life.

Business cards were made for those who wanted to share the book with a link to purchase it so we could pass them out to everyone we knew. I was passionate about sharing my card and the book with everyone I met.

An idea was suggested to hold a party at our house to share the exercises with everyone we knew. It was springtime, and we had a nice yard to have everyone and a basement to set up space for a presentation. I invited everyone we knew by text, email, and Facebook.

"Randy, do you think you could teach the exercises for the *Solar Body* Party? I'll do the presentation and help you set up, but I think it's best for you to teach," I asked.

"Sure, I can do it. No problem."

We set up our basement with chairs and a laptop to show the presentation we were given about the book and exercises. Neighbors, friends, and family came. I shared my story about all the changes I experienced with this book and these 3 exercises.

"I feel less stressed, and my body feels so much better. I have been doing these three exercises daily for 60 days, and my whole life has changed. I was suffering with extreme acid indigestion, taking prescription medications and supplements, and watching what I ate. Nothing helped. I slept in a chair most nights, desperate with the acid taste in my throat. My bowel movements fluctuated between constipation and diarrhea. I couldn't hold my head straight and was in constant pain in my shoulders and neck. Now I'm taking fewer meds for my digestion since it's gotten better and I'm sleeping through the night. My shoulder and neck pain are improving, and my digestion is more regular. I'm feeling so much better."

As I spoke these words like some type of advertisement, feeling the amazement myself, I could see the expressions on Teresa's and Randy's faces. Tears were welling up in Teresa's eyes as she listened intently. The look of disbelief and amazement on Randy's face brought emotion up for me, but I had to keep talking, choking back my tears. They were my support system and had seen me at my most desperate times.

After the presentation, we went in the yard for the exercises. Randy set up music and a speaker for the class and towels and mats for when it was time to lie down. Our yard was full of our friends, family, and neighbors gathered in a circle to do *Solar Body* Exercises with us.

Randy was comfortable teaching right away. There was some giggling and chatter at first, but as the exercises got more involved, everyone quieted down. Coming down to the towels on the grass was a challenge for some.

Leeta, who had been teaching and had a center of her own in Chicago, was there to help us. She helped guide people individually with some of the exercises. Her nature was always patient and caring.

I also helped where I could, mostly watching in amazement and taking pictures and video. I could see everyone was feeling the benefits of the exercises, breathing out and their faces starting to relax.

After the class, people shared, "I feel so relaxed. My shoulders feel looser, and it's easier to take a deep breath."

Our *Solar Body* Party was a success! A few people bought books and inquired about classes too, and we told them about Mt. Prospect Body & Brain center where we were members.

"That was so nice to have everyone here at the house. You did a great job teaching the exercises. Everyone seemed to enjoy it," I said to Randy.

"Yes, it was great to have everyone here. I liked teaching too."

I was feeling so grateful for all the changes I was feeling from classes and the *Solar Body* exercises I did at home that I wanted to share it with others. We had a fitness center in the basement of the Salvation Army Headquarters where I worked. There was a space for a class in the fitness center, which was away from all the machines. I asked the woman who oversaw the fitness center if I could offer a short class at lunchtime, so I could share these *Solar Body* exercises. She agreed, and I was teaching a few people in the gym and talking to everyone I knew about Body & Brain and how great it was for me. There were several people that came and went from the classes I offered. It was good practice for me.

My coworker Diane stuck with me the most, and we exercised together at breaks and lunch. We also had a walking track and an outside grassy area where we had lunch and exercised, too. It was the beginning of my sharing what I learned with others. Diane became a long-time member of Body & Brain in Mt. Prospect, feeling the benefits of the classes. She retired and moved away and now joins them online.

Brain Management Training

♥

What if that change you're avoiding is the one that gives you wings?

June 4th, 2015:

Brain Management Training was our next training in Sedona. This training was recommended to help learn to manage our brain daily. Realizing how attached we were to each other, we agreed, after some advice, to room with others for this training so I could focus on myself more. This was a big challenge for me but something I felt was necessary for my growth. Randy was hesitant also, but we agreed it would be good for our growth.

Before going to BMT I wrote in my journal about my fears.

May 30 Journal Entry:

"I have so much attachment to Randy; I'm afraid to be alone. I'm always attached to someone. I know it's good for both of us. We need to grow separately so we can practice together, but it's so difficult to do. We have been connected at the hip until now. Each step seems so hard at the beginning, but then it gets easier once things are put into perspective."

June 24th:

What must people think? I feel so different now. Do I act different? Why does she want to room with me? I guess I should just go along. My old self would want to be comfortable and room with Randy, but in my heart, I know I need to do this to give myself a chance to grow. I've always depended on him or someone else for comfort and haven't had the opportunity to depend on myself. *Maybe it will help me.*

In hindsight, rooming with someone else enabled me to grow a lot.

I did realize how attached I was to Randy and why it might be necessary for my growth.

I shared a room with a woman who would have liked to spend more time together, but I wanted to do my own thing. This was time to be by myself and find my individuality. I wanted to take advantage of the time there for myself.

I woke up early, and I would walk to the healing garden, my favorite spot. The air was crisp, the sky was bright blue with picture perfect puffs of clouds. Birds sang for me, and the scents of lavender and rosemary filled the air. The lake rippled with the breeze as ducks floated by. This was heaven on earth.

For the first time ever, I enjoyed my time alone and followed my own pace and going to places when I felt the need and wandering around this beautiful place with so much natural beauty and healing energy. I was learning to trust myself. It was the beginning of my individuality and friendship with myself. I started to blossom into my own person, not just being a wife, mom, or friend, but my true self.

We learned many helpful self-care techniques and I couldn't wait to share them with my friends and family when I got back home.

The opportunity was presented on the last day to run a franchise at home. Watching the presentation on the screen about others having space in their homes for a studio immediately woke up excitement in my whole body. My heart began to pound with joy at the possibility of this. We had a finished, empty basement that could be transformed to a center. As the tears flowed down my cheeks, the creation of this dream began.

Rushing over to Randy after the presentation was over, ready to burst with excitement, "I really want to do this. What do you think?"

"We'll talk about it. Let's get more information." He answered with possibility.

This in-home studio franchise was what I wanted more than anything in the world at this moment. I could help others grow and change, which I had experienced myself. I had to follow this dream!

After going back to reality and work I was excited to share more.

Before Body & Brain, I had taken yoga classes for several years with friends, and alone sometimes, since I felt the need for something to relax. I enjoyed the classes doing the yoga poses and sun salutations but was never able to quiet my brain at relaxation time. I was always thinking of what I needed to do next or what else was going on with the kids or my family.

I admired the teacher. She was very, kind, and gentle in her mannerisms and guidance. Her voice was soft, which helped me feel relaxed. She was always dressed simply, no make- up and hair in one even layer. I enjoyed the energy and wisdom she shared through the exercises.

One evening, the thought came to mind about how nice it might be to become a yoga teacher, just like her. After class, I asked her how long it took to get her yoga teaching certification. She said something like 9 months or so. I was an accounting clerk at the time with the Salvation Army, so I didn't see any way to make it happen. The thought came and went quickly.

Now I had the opportunity to teach yoga. The seed was planted in my subconscious and now it was coming to fruition.

Sharing 7/14/15:

I'm excited to be sharing with others at work. I feel so much energy and love at times. I'm amazed at my own growth. I can't believe how far I've come. It's hard to trust what I don't see. People react to me differently. I feel more connected to my core and heart, and my soul is happy. I'm getting healthier. I'm trying to help others and lead them. It is awkward when I think about the cost. Our hearts know the truth, but our brain judges and mistrusts. I have so much attachment to money.

Starting to Teach at Work

♥

8 /9/15

    I taught two classes today at the Salvation Army Headquarters. I enjoyed connecting with others. I'm nervous about the ability to handle all of it. I'm worried about others and their thoughts. I feel so disconnected sometimes. I feel better after connecting with others. Will I be able to handle all the ups and downs and the time commitment to running our own business? My heart is ready, but my brain isn't. My brain worries and considers worldly problems.

    I was taught to identify feelings as owning them instead of being them. Hence, I say I have these feelings, not I am....... This separates our feelings from who we are. Our true nature is pure and bright. These thoughts and feelings are like clouds covering our beautiful heart, -the sun which always exists.

    There's always two sides of a dream and growth. There is the excitement and fear and challenges. The deeper we go, the muddier the emotions are.

    9/1/15:

    I have loneliness. I have confusion. I have impatience. I have fear. I don't trust. I want others to do things for me. I don't want to work hard. I don't trust. I have frustration. I want to avoid difficulties.

When I am full of love and acceptance, I find peace. I will always be uneasy when I'm away from my true nature and who I really am.

9/13/15:

I have so much anger and disappointment. I have anger when people don't do as I please. I have frustration. I have blame. I have hatred. I have loneliness. I am afraid of being alone. I have a fear that he will wander away. I want to be loved for who I am.

I can't expect anything from anyone anymore. The only one I can count on is me. I will lose myself when I count on others for anything. I create my own happiness. Nobody can do that for me. His ego gets in my way. His heart is genuine, but his ego is so strong. I am responsible for myself. I depended on his comfort for so long, and I'm afraid to be without it. The past is gone, and things will no longer be the same. I must follow my heart now. No more attachments. My heart will be my comfort. I must be strong.

I follow my emotions and get carried away. All is well. I have a wonderful life, and I make it negative. There are two ways to see things, always positive or negative. I have dissatisfaction instead of gratitude. I will overcome my doubt and become a good teacher and healer. All I need is practice. It's just another thing to accept about myself. I am love and light. My true nature is love, acceptance, gratitude, light, and nature.

9/15:

I attended the Finding True Self workshop again today. It was so nice to share a common passion with others. It felt great to be part of the community. I realized I was wrong to be so arrogant to my family. They loved me the best way they knew how. My parents gave me life, and I didn't appreciate it.

I Want to Fly

♥

The butterfly does not look back upon its caterpillar self, it simply flies on.

When we got back from Brain Management Training, I found out the information about owning a franchise and I was ready to take the leap. Randy and I originally planned for him to continue to work, and I would run the center in our basement. It turned out he wasn't working at the time so we were both going to run the center to get started and we would just work things out as they went along.

I was working at Salvation Army near my home for 12 years and running out of vacation time. I had been to Sedona a few times the previous year for different trainings and needed to go to Dahn Master & BBC CEO before we could open our franchise.

I had no doubt about what I wanted to do, now I had to let my boss know. He knew how involved I was with my Body & Brain practice and how much it helped me.

"I would like to give my two weeks' notice. I will be opening a yoga studio at my home. My last day will be September 30."

"Okay, I'm not surprised JoAnn. I wish you the best. We will miss you as part of our team. Are you sure this is what you want to do?"

"Yes, this practice has changed my life, and I want to share it with others now. There's not any reluctance at all. Thank you for everything.

I will do my best to show Diane everything I do so she can train the next person."

I'm doing this. I can't believe it, but I can't ignore my heart. I have to keep going toward my dream now. I thought as I triumphantly went back to my office.

Salvation Army Headquarters, where I worked, had announced one year before they would move to a new location about 20 miles away. I was less than two miles from the current location. I had always worked close to home, so when the move was announced, I had it in my mind that I wouldn't go with them. My last day of work was the day before the company moved. I left for Dahn Master's training a couple days after that.

My siblings and our kids were concerned about this choice we were making to leave our "secure" jobs and start a business at almost sixty years old.

"JoAnn, are you sure this is a good idea?" my brother David asked. "Do you and Randy know what you're doing? What about retirement? Do you have money saved for this?"

"Yes, it's what we want, and we believe it will work out. I feel so much better than before, so I want to share it with others."

Our eldest son became the nervous parent and was genuinely concerned about what we were doing. "Do you guys have a business plan? Are you sure about this? How does it work? How much does it cost, and how much can you earn?"

I suppose they had valid points to be concerned about, but in my mind, there was no question I had to do this.

"I trust it will work out. Our heart is in the right place. It's helped me so much. Don't you notice how much I changed?"

I had to share with others about Body & Brain principles and exercises. I believed so strongly that I needed to do this since I had experienced so much change in my life. I never had a doubt in my mind once I made this decision.

"I read some stuff about Body & Brain. Are you sure this is a good idea?" Nick asked.

"I'm proud of you both. I'm sure you'll do great," Teresa encouraged.

Being the outspoken one, I said, "This is something I want to do, and I trust it will work out because we have good intentions. I know you don't understand, but I know in my heart it's what I want to do."

"We are opening a franchise and will get a lot of support from Body & Brain. There is another franchise center in Bloomingdale, and she's been very successful. She's ten years older than us." I shared.

Dahn Master Training

♥

I am Heaven, Earth, and Human; this is my promise

October 2015

I always imagined Dahn Master training would be physically challenging, testing my strength and character to the utmost. Becoming a Dahn Master sounded quite honorable. Dahn means energy, and I would become an energy master. Once we completed the training, we would go to Korea for a graduation ceremony to receive our uniforms.

My life had already changed in many ways, and my heart guided me to become a Dahn Master. I was preparing to start my journey of being a mentor instead of the mentee. Each training I participated in, I learned more about myself and gathered tools for sharing and guiding others.

I always used the analogy of Body & Brain being my college education which I never had. What better way to spend money than to improve myself emotionally, spiritually, and physically?

Randy & I took the training and roomed together. We were becoming vision partners with one common goal.

Being in Sedona Mago was like going back home once again. I connected to the beautiful nature, energy, and myself. Even though we roomed together I went for walks on my own and ate with others in the dining room. We were individuals now, and no longer needed to be together constantly. This was growth we both needed.

Dahn Master was a very deep spiritual training. I became more connected to my divine nature and felt my energy becoming purer and one with the universe. We rose early in the morning to start our day and the training went until late.

Learning about our significant role in sharing the Hongik Vision with others reminded me of who I was. The Hongik Vision means to benefit all, not just myself. This vision touched my soul deeply.

Through this training I embodied Heaven and Earth making a promise to my soul to live for this purpose. It is perfectly said in the poem Prayer of Peace.

I'd like to share the Prayer of Peace by Ilchi Lee that was shared at the United Nations Millennium World Peace Summit of Religious and Spiritual Leaders August 28, 2000, as a vision of peace that transcends religious, racial, and national boundaries.

Reading this message resonated with me deeply.

Prayer of Peace

I offer this prayer of peace
   Not to the Christian God
   Nor to the Buddhist God
   Nor to the Islamic God
   Nor to the Jewish God
   But to the God of all humanity.
   For the peace that we wish for
   Is not a Christian peace
   Nor a Buddhist peace
   Nor an Islamic peace
   Nor a Jewish peace
   But a human peace
   For all of us.
   I offer this prayer of peace
   To the God that lives within all of us
   That fills us with happiness and joy

To make us whole
And help us understand life
As an expression of love for all human beings
For no religion can be better
Than any other religion
For no truth can be truer
Than any other truth
For no nation can be bigger
Than the Earth itself.
Help us all go beyond
Our small limits
And realize that we are one
That we are all from the Earth
That we are all Earth People
Before we are Indians, Koreans, or Americans.
God made the Earth
We humans have to make it prosper
By realizing that we are of the Earth
And not of any nation, race, or religion,
By knowing that we are truly one
In our spiritual heritage.
Let us now apologize
To all humanity
For the hurt that religions have caused,
So that we can heal the hurt.
Let us now promise to one another
To go beyond egotism and competition
To come together as one in God.
I offer this prayer of peace
To you the almighty
To help us find you within all of us
So that we may stand proudly
One day before you
As one humanity.

I offer this prayer of peace
With all my fellow Earth People
For a lasting peace on Earth.

Chopping Wood, Carrying Water

♥

Progress is a process. –Kevin Deshazo

When I returned from Dahn Master, I began to work at Mt. Prospect Body & Brain under Magdalena. She was the center manager and taught me discipline, integrity, and accountability. She was stern but encouraging at the same time. Working under her, I learned what it took to work with people, accept disappointments when people changed their minds or couldn't decide, and get up and keep going to find the next person we could help. The time I spent working there was invaluable. I needed to learn all of this before BBC CEO training and opening my in-home center.

Randy had originally planned to continue to work while I ran the home center. He ended up leaving his job before me because they were way too demanding of his time. He couldn't turn his back on what he was waking up to and didn't want to give up taking classes and trainings himself. He also worked at Mount Prospect center teaching classes and passing out brochures for them as training before our center opening.

I learned how to do advertising and administrative duties, such as sending emails to members, making monthly class calendars, and scheduling and conducting introductory sessions. This on-the-job training lasted for about six months or so.

We were still getting paid working part time there while training, but it was going to take all our energy and effort to get our home center going.

Franchise Training

♥

D ecember 2015

We went back to the Sedona Mago Center to learn the logistics of running our center. Lots of doubt and fear came up for both of us as we learned everything from answering calls, aura reading, introductory sessions to making a monthly plan to grow our business. There was a small group of 5 people for this training who were planning to open a franchise or working in corporate centers. During the training, we demonstrated introductory sessions and answering the phone and aura readings. We didn't feel as comfortable as we would like to be. It made us nervous.

Starting to feel the reality of what we were getting into, we began to argue more, worrying about how things would be. "Maybe I should look for a job, and you run the center like you planned," Randy would say.

"You said you wanted to do this together, but now you're changing your mind. You need to decide and stick to it. I know you're scared about not having the steady income, but we have to trust it will work out," I argued.

We worked together and raised a family together. *Could we run a business together?*

Sometimes I would feel excited about my new journey.

Journal entry December 2015:

"I have grown so much in the last 16 months. I'm amazed with myself. My heart has opened wide, and I feel free from all my self judgement. I'm ready to begin my new life!"

Travelling Solo!

Challenges are opportunities for growth!

Travelling to Sedona Mago Retreat many times with Randy, I never went alone. There was a Personal Coaching Program I wanted to take before opening our center. I felt it was something I needed to do on my own. This was an opportunity to further my growth and independence.

I signed up and made the reservations for myself to attend. We usually rented a car with Randy driving from the airport. Mago Garden is 1 ½ hours from the airport, and I wouldn't drive on my own, so I arranged to take the shuttle instead.

Anxiety about travelling alone and being away from Randy and my family for a week stirred. The journey there was challenging, travelling alone, waiting for the shuttle. I wasn't used to being alone. Sedona Mago Retreat Center was familiar to me, so I knew I'd be comfortable once I was there. Carrying a small stone I bought somewhere that said "Strength," I would hold the stone and affirm, "I am strong."

I had a wide variety of emotions. I felt strong, confident, and able. I also had loneliness and fear. I was far away from the outside world, which brought up different feelings. I told myself, I will accept the disconnect from the world back home and soak in the healing of nature.

The inner struggle was there.

Journal Entry First night:

What am I doing here? I feel so disconnected from my family at home. I hope Teresa and the baby are okay. I feel guilty not being there when she's having trouble with her pregnancy. I have been so busy with my new life and growing and learning. I feel out of touch. I hope she and the baby are okay. She is usually difficult to reach unless she is ready. She's independent that way. Now I am working on myself, someday I hope she can do the same.

It's so beautiful and peaceful here, yet I feel so lonely and lost. It's okay to feel my emotions. They are mine, but not me. My old self comes up being needy and lonely, but I am strong. I can take care of myself. I have a habit of regret and worry, negative thinking. If my thinking was more of acceptance and being present, I would feel better. I'd be more grounded. I want to heal myself from negative thoughts.

There were others there for the same training that I connected with but didn't depend on as I would have done in the past. I had a roommate, and we visited while in the room, but I felt a sense of independence at the same time. I was happy to be on my own, which was different from any experience I ever had in my life. I was grateful to be okay by myself!

I was happy to go to the dining hall on my own and get to class on my own. I also enjoyed taking breaks and doing what I enjoyed in my free time. Before Body & Brain, I would want to be with someone all the time. Now I cherished my alone time. I felt like a different person from the inside. I felt strong. I was home again in this beautiful place, the home of my soul.

Journal entry 3rd night:

Started to feel sick and tired today. I was enjoying my time until I spoke to Randy. I started thinking about life at home. What's going to happen? I get so anxious about things. I worry about my body. I am afraid for my body. I feel my body is me. I have felt my heart but can't keep that focus. I'm tired of running away, pretending all is well. I wish I could get my point across to others, but I can't change anyone. Will I be successful? I'm not sure.

3/6 My last night of health coaching:

This was my first trip to Sedona alone. I did fine. I did feel lonely at times for Randy and my family. It's such a wonderful place here away from everything. It's so beautiful and peaceful here. It feels like a home away from home. I enjoyed the training. I learned a lot about myself. I still have fear, but I'm able to move forward. It was hard giving feedback to others in class, but I realized it's easier when given with a sincere heart.

I learned a lot during the classes about coaching people. The main take away is to listen and ask questions so they can come up with their own answers. People need to hear themselves and usually they can figure out the answers after they connect to themselves on a deeper level. This can be done through exercises and breathing to quiet the thinking brain and wake up the subconscious.

This was a great training before opening the business for several reasons. I became stronger travelling on my own, learned more tools to help myself and others, and I learned how to present myself as a coach with an outline and program to follow. This was my jumping board to begin Body & Brain Yoga Tai Chi Des Plaines.

Des Plaines Center Opening

♥

Journal about all your worries to unbury your soul's voice.

I t was April 2016, and it was time to start making some income on our own. We planned a grand opening event and invited everyone we knew. Our families and friends were there to support us in this new venture. We were both in our early 50s when we started our Health, Happiness, and Peace LLC. Our adult children were genuinely concerned about us doing this, worried that we didn't have enough of a plan or money to start our business and had no idea what it would take to run a business.

Of course, I was worried too. There were times before bed I would journal pages of what ifs and making members and getting money to pay our bills.

Doubt and Fear Journal Entry 4/14:

"What if nobody wants to take our classes? What if we can't make enough money to support ourselves? What if things just don't work out?

After all these worries and what ifs came out, the thought of what if we succeed arose? What if we help lots of people?

What if it all works out and we do great?

This epiphany came as sunshine after the clouds of fears had passed and released through my journaling.

Randy has always been handy around the house, so he did the painting for the center and all the work himself. I ordered and planned the simple furniture and ordered the banners for the walls. We had a 10x4-foot area separated by dark wood shoji screens set up as our lobby at the bottom of the stairs. There was an antique desk with a lamp, two chairs, hooks on the wall for jackets, and a small rug for shoes. On the other side of the shoji screen was a 10x12-foot area with 6 ½ foot ceilings which were a bit low for tall people. We installed a padded floor made of wood looking like puzzle tiles and yellow walls. The blue Life Particle Sun banner and Chun Bu Kyung were hung on the wall.

Our grand opening was kind of a success, considering we had many people attend. The grand opening was inside the house and in the yard. We had discounts and raffles for mindfulness books, classes, and private sessions. There were signs and balloons out in front of the house. Free class was in the yard and Aura Reading in the kitchen. Small sandwiches, salads and cookies and lemon water were served as well. We wore teachers' clothes now including (Hanbok) which means Korean tops and loose-fitting yoga pants.

The only purchase made was by a woman who was taking classes at a Senior Center where Randy taught a weekly class for the Seniors. He started teaching this class from Mt. Prospect Center and continued from our Des Plaines Center. She brought her husband for the event. She inquired, "Can we share a 5-class card?"

In disbelief, I choked out the words, "I guess so. Wouldn't you both like five classes?"

"I'm not sure how often we will take classes. George is still working."

"Ok, that's fine." I succumbed.

We had spent a lot of money and energy and this event providing snacks, decorations, and this was the only person who wanted to purchase anything. I was insulted by the nerve of this woman.

What were we doing? Was this really a mistake? Maybe everyone was right.

These questions began to arise after the open house, but I tried not to let it bother me. On one hand, we felt this was a sign of something wasn't right. On the other hand, it was just the beginning, and we had to keep going. We had to find new people that felt the value in what we were teaching. In the beginning, I spent a lot of time with friends and anyone who wanted to try coaching sessions or energy healing so I could practice and gain their trust and my own confidence. Looking back, I feel grateful for our first members giving us a chance by trying classes and coaching sessions. When people felt better after a session or class, I started to gain more confidence.

I was learning that I had to keep going no matter what. We both had to accept the triumphs and losses.

People would schedule appointments over the phone. "Yes, I'll be there at 2pm. I'll pay when I get there." I would prepare my mind and space for them, and they wouldn't show up. These feelings of being stood up were particularly challenging for me. It brought up memories of my friend not wanting to play with me and going somewhere else to see another friend.

What's wrong? Did I say or not say something to cause them to not show up? I questioned and blamed myself.

The emotions reminded me of my teen years. I was hurt many times. I always felt that others didn't like me, or I wasn't good enough. I felt this same let down, like when people didn't come when they said they would or didn't call as promised.

However, at this time, I also realized this may be part of business and my own growth and healing. I had to accept these disappointments and not judge from a personal point of view.

Eventually, after trial and error, hurts and disappointments, we started to gather members for coaching sessions first and then group classes.

I always enjoyed connecting with people on a deeper level, and now I had tools to help them with their struggles.

We had a separate room for private sessions in the back area of the basement. There was a dark brown corduroy couch we would sit on to talk about their goals and background. A heated mat was on the floor with a small pillow and soft blanket that was used for simple exercises to relax the body and energy healing. Colorful bird puzzles were displayed on the walls and the Chun Bu Kyung an ancient scripture in gold characters, which was given from Mt. Prospect Center to us, and some dark wood Asian cabinets.

Once I sensed what they needed, we would exercise together. Next, they laid on the warm mat, and I would send energy to their chakras to help them open and balance their qi (or ki).

Tears would flow, breath would get deeper, and sometimes they would fall asleep. When the session was done, they would express they didn't want to leave. People would share about the positive changes they felt after our sessions, like they were more relaxed and felt better about themselves. I was making a difference in people's lives with the tools I learned and love I shared.

We did whatever we could to get the word out about our home business. The only way people knew we existed was through social media, networking, and brochures. Randy always has and still loves passing out brochures, door-to-door. I was the one in charge or our online presence, and I still oversee our social media and networking. After a couple months of mostly private sessions, we started to gather people for classes.

Randy taught a lot of the classes when we started, so I would wait upstairs until everyone came in. I would go down to take pictures briefly during class to use for advertising.

Those first piles of shoes on the small rug in the lobby area brought up tears of joy. I was thrilled we had members for class in our basement center.

That first year was the most challenging, adjusting to making all of our own money.

Randy drove for Uber and did some job searching that first year when income was low and business was slow. At one point, we agreed that if we trusted and focused all our energy on the business things would pick up. He stopped the driving for Uber and job search, and everything began to improve.

We held aura reading events at different places to meet new people. The Vitamin Shoppe has always welcomed Body & Brain for aura reading, which helped us many times to meet new people.

I started to teach more of the classes at home, and I was enjoying connecting with the members and doing private sessions as well.

Randy was given the opportunity to teach a class at a few senior community centers and assisted living facilities, and I volunteered to teach a class monthly at a local nursing home. These classes were special. Teaching and interacting with people close to my parents' age warmed my heart. Some of the women reminded me of my mom, who had passed. The way they spoke or looked frequently brought tears to my eyes remembering her. The people at the nursing home really appreciated me coming in to teach the class for them. I was happy to have a positive influence in their day. We also taught classes at library events, church groups, and even the Barefoot Hawaiian dance studio.

The members at our home center started to build relationships with each other and had a place to come to feel better in body and mind.

One of my neighbors, Mary Lou, who came for class regularly, called our house "the healing house."

While helping others improve their health and well-being, we also enjoyed getting to know many people, young and old.

When the weather was nice, we had classes outside in our yard and at Lake Opeka. Being in our yard under the tree or by the lake at sunset for class was always healing.

We gathered groups for Sedona Meditation Tours, Energy Healing Course, and Brain Management Training. Members took Initial Awakening, Finding True Self and encouraged and supported each other to participate in workshops.

"The workshop was amazing. I realized things about myself and my relationships that I never knew about. I feel so much better about myself. Everyone should take it," they would share about Finding True Self.

Randy also taught a class at a karate studio on the northwest side of Chicago, recommended by someone from Mount Prospect center. Over the years, the members brought friends and enjoyed the benefits from class and helped support our business. These were his members that he created since he taught those classes regularly. I was happy for him to have this space to expand his reach on his own. Chicago was his territory for now.

Our relationship had evolved from romance to parenting, with some co-dependency, to a business partnership as true soulmates. We found our purpose in life together.

New Stress, Old Friend

After a few months of our new business, my cervical dystonia came back. I believe it was due to all the stress of leaving the security of a steady income and giving so much time and energy to our new business. Now I really understood how much my body reacted to stress. I had to schedule appointments and classes at least one hour apart so I could rest on the couch in between.

Our beige leather couch upstairs was worn in the center from where my bottom rested, as I rested my head on the armrest.

Other center managers that I had become close to along with Randy were concerned about me and saw how much pain I had to endure. Any time I was sitting unsupported in meetings or workshops, I grimaced and writhed in pain.

After months of suffering, one day I was talking on the phone with Ji-hee, another franchise owner, whom I had become close to. She checked in with me regularly and was always very supportive. Knowing how much pain I was in, one day she said to me, "Why don't you just let Randy run the center?"

Shocked by this suggestion, I snapped back, "No way. I can't just lay on the couch all day. This is My Dream."

Remembering how excited I was from the moment I heard about the home center franchise, I would not give up and let him take over.

Somehow, I knew I had to keep going. I trusted that what I was doing was right, and eventually I would get better again. I couldn't give up now.

A member once said to me during a private session, "I'll do that training after I lose weight and don't have pain in my knees."

I answered, "If I waited until my neck was better, I would not be here with you." Many times, words like these came from my mouth without a filter.

I gave my all to each member, wanting to help them feel better. Words came to help them to hear what they needed, and I learned from them as well.

Even though I suffered from this chronic pain, I enjoyed connecting with people and helping them improve their lives.

Trip to Korea

♥

A trip was planned to Korea in October 2016 to receive our Dahn Master uniforms. Visiting the country where Body & Brain began brought up excitement and some concerns. The trip was twelve days long, and we would have to leave our center after gaining momentum with new members coming for classes.

My cervical dystonia was painful, but this trip was important, so we wanted to go.

First, we attended the First National Qigong Festival. Thousands of people filled the stadium with passion and excitement. Arms waved through the air as happy Korean songs were played on the sound system. Many carefully choreographed Kigong performances in beautiful costumes from all around the world filled the stage. The energy was exciting and fun. I was amazed to realize how many countries were represented at this event. We all spoke different languages, but our smiles and bright eyes reflected our joy to be part of this worldwide community.

We travelled by bus to a few different areas in Korea. Staying at Kookhak Wan, a cultural training center Ilchi Lee created, was another special time.

Sleeping arrangements consisted of a mattress with two small pillows on a wooden floor. There was no furniture and only essentials, including toiletries in the bathroom adjacent. We each had an open cubby to hang our clothes and keep our suitcases. The simple setup was quite comfortable. I remember a large statue of a bird lit up outside our window. I slept well each night after full days of travel, training, and sightseeing. Resting my heavy head on the pillow at night was my respite.

Toward the end of the trip, we arrived at the place where the graduation ceremony would take place. We would receive our uniforms from a senior Taoist master named Manwol. Ilchi Lee appointed Manwol to give the uniforms to the Dahn Master graduates. I always envied others who had their uniforms, which consisted of a button-down, cream-colored top with navy blue trim and navy loose-fitting pants. Now it was time to receive mine. It was a special day for me to receive this uniform to represent my divine nature and purpose. There were about fifteen of us from all around the world here to receive our Dahn Master uniforms. We were called up one by one to receive our uniforms.

"JoAnn Dickson" I walked slowly up the stairs and Manwol, half bowing in front of me, presented the carefully folded cream colored with navy trim button-down shirt to me. Receiving this uniform felt honorable.

I sincerely received the shirt, weeping with joy. Her gentle embrace filled my body with loving energy as my heart opened to hers.

Tears streaming down my cheeks as I bowed, expressing my gratitude to her and for this most special moment in my life. "Kahnsamnida". (Thank you)

Lots of tears and congratulatory hugs were exchanged after the ceremony, along with pictures and dancing. We had all received our Dahn Master uniforms and would go home to begin a new life based on our promises.

Overwhelmed with gratitude and joy, I graduated as a Dahn Master. This event also represented the beginning of my new life.

The trip home was long. We had experienced the Korean culture, the Hongik Vision (to benefit all) and the Graduation Ceremony.

Arriving home, we started teaching classes again, now with newfound strength and energy as Dahn Masters. Seeing our members again brought up our grateful hearts.

We were also looking forward to seeing our family again after our long trip. Teresa had a family get together and made us a Congratulations Dahn Master card and everyone signed it! We were thrilled with the thought of our children being supportive of our dream.

We visited my dad also, a few days after coming back. We brought pizza and watched car shows with him in the living room. It was good to see him, too.

End of Life Crisis?

♥

M y dad was lost and lonely without my mom to take care of. After a couple years of mourning his loss, he decided to buy himself a brand new 2017 Camaro Convertible. This was something he couldn't have purchased with my mom around. She would never agree to this type of car. At 92 years old, maybe he was having an end-of-life crisis?

Driving down the street in his flashy white convertible, he got a lot of attention. We knew it was a matter of time before something serious would happen. It seemed impossible to take his keys and car while he was well enough to drive.

We visited on weekends, usually bringing pizza for lunch. He was sitting on the porch listening to Dean Martin on his boombox when we arrived. After a few minutes, he told us the police had just left. He explained someone next to him at a stoplight was asking him about his car and he backed up to talk and bumped into the car behind him. He panicked and left the scene before the police arrived. The police warned him about being more careful and not to leave when something happens like that next time. He was lucky he didn't get arrested. We were concerned about his safety and the safety of others with him driving, but none of us knew what to do.

Becoming an Orphan

❤

One summer evening, while closing the front door of his home, dad tripped on a throw rug and fell and broke his hip. He had to go to a nursing home where he could be cared for after having surgery. This was the end of his last hurrah with his sports car. He was devastated. He begged to just see his car once again. My sister, who oversaw his care, thought it was best that he didn't see the car. She knew it would create more trouble since he couldn't drive anymore. It was parked in my sister's son Joey's garage.

Randy and I visited weekly, having lunch in the dining room with him and sometimes listening to a piano player in the common area with him. While sitting together listening to the music, he would cry and cry, holding his face in his hands.

All that remained of his life was his bed, dresser, recliner, chair, and clothes. He had an 8x10 picture of his Camaro, a 16x20 of him and my mom with lip marks from kissing her good night, and pictures of us and my sister's family with all the grandkids.

When we visited, he reminisced about his life and him updating the house I grew up in and the cars he owned over the years. He talked about my mom and how they went to the roller rink when they were dating and being married for 67 years.

He was proud of us having our home business and asked frequently how it was going. My cervical dystonia was bad at this time, and he would look at me with concern and ask if I was ok. I would try to change the subject quickly. "I'm fine. It's just the way it is."

One day Randy and he were talking, and my dad expressed wanting to make amends with my brother David. Randy dialed the phone for my dad, and the answering machine came on. My dad left a message saying he just wanted to talk. My brother couldn't forget how he was rejected after my mom's death, so he blocked my dad's number so he couldn't call again. I was happy my father was ready to let go before he passed, but sad it was too late for my brother to forgive him.

My dad was humbler and more sensitive than ever, which made me feel closer to him. Being an ex-smoker, he loved to have toothpicks to chew on or hang from his mouth after his meals. He complained they didn't have any toothpicks where he was staying. The next time, I brought him a small round dispenser with toothpicks, and he was thrilled by this small gesture.

My father was the sole supporter of our family growing up, while working as a truck mechanic. He did his best with what he knew, never realizing how blessed he was with his family. On April 3, 2018, he turned 93. Then, on Mother's Day, he died of kidney failure.

Now I was an orphan. Even though I complained about my parents and didn't appreciate them as I should have, they were my parents. They always cared about me and had my best interest in mind. There's nobody that can ever replace them. I'm forever grateful to them for giving me life and a secure environment to grow up in.

Is it my turn yet?

♥

"Where your mind goes, energy flows."

- Brain Operating System by Ilchi Lee

I had been invited to a group training program within Body & Brain because of our successful business model for a home center. I was also working with a woman named Oceana privately online to help me with my challenges and self-development. She knew how much pain I had endured with cervical dystonia and my heart to help others. One day she said she would contact someone about my condition and see how it could be improved. She tried many ways to help me emotionally and physically to feel better, but I still suffered.

Randy and I wanted to expand our business. We were able to touch many lives from our home center, but there were limits. Our dream was a storefront center with a door to the public so people could stop in to see us, with signs all around, and with high enough ceilings for tall people, and with space for more than six people. While dealing with the chronic pain, it would be too much for me to handle.

Ilchi Lee was always coming up with new ideas for self-healing. Currently, he was teaching Brain Energy Healing Points (BHP), which are acupressure points in the brain that correspond to various parts of the body.

During one of our group meetings, I learned BHP directly from Ilchi Lee.

At other trainings over the years, many people had been asked to go in front for a demonstration. I always longed for the day when it would be my turn. I had been desperate to feel better.

I went up and sat in a chair in front of many of my peers within Body & Brain. Ilchi Lee guided me on where to stimulate the Brain Energy Healing Points. They were very sensitive, and it amazed me how much I felt by pressing them. I'm certain it was a short amount of time, but it seemed like an eternity. I couldn't bear it for long. As I sat there with the sensation fading, Ilchi Lee began to speak to me. "JoAnn has been suffering for a long time. Her heart says, I'm so desperate. I don't know what to do. I can't live like this anymore. I have a vision to help others, but some days I can't bear the pain. Someone, please help me."

Sobbing in front of everyone uncontrollably, these unspoken thoughts were mine. My deep pain was being exposed to all. The room of 100 people or more became silent. I composed myself after the sobs slowed down. I was given tissues to wipe my tears and long holding hugs by the translator and Ilchi Lee. I thanked him several times, bowing to him with profound gratitude. As I got up from the chair, my pain was gone, and my head was straight.

I couldn't express the honor I felt for this opportunity. He spoke through translation, "I want you to feel better and be relieved of your suffering. It brings me joy to help you." These words he spoke to me were my wish to other people that I worked with as well. Emotion flooded my body again, realizing we were the same. I recognized at that moment how much joy I felt to help others feel better physically and emotionally. And the tools I used, I learned through my own healing and experiences with Body & Brain. Therefore, I chose and continue to be a center manager, teacher, and coach. Yes, we have the same heart to help others.

Gratefully and amazingly, my condition slowly and gradually improved from this point forward. I did BHP for myself daily and increased Chun Mun meditation, which is balancing an object such as a stone from Sedona that I had collected on top of my head to receive energy. This practice would also help strengthen and straighten my cervical spine. After a few months, my pain and posture improved significantly.

Members, family, and other center managers were noticing a remarkable change in my appearance. My head was much straighter than before, and I didn't have to hold my head up with my hand while talking or sitting unsupported.

Seeing my shadow on the ground with my head straight meant the world to me. I couldn't believe my eyes and the feeling of my condition. After all the pain and struggles, I was strong again and in control of the posture of my head.

More energy and passion for our business was emerging from within now that my condition had improved. This meant we could open a storefront center.

Although we thought we were ready for this growth, the process was challenging. There were a lot of logistics to finding a location. We wanted to be close to Chicago but not too far from our home, and we had to have a 10-mile radius from the other Body & Brain centers in the Chicago area. The grueling search went on for about six months. Lots of car trips, phone calls, and research. We found a place in Edison Park and River Grove, which we were excited about until they fell through. We had our minds set on each of those places and were ready to begin until zoning and handicap bathroom rules stopped us from proceeding.

Photographs

♥

Siblings

My parents with my sister and I

Me as a teen

Family

Randy and I on our wedding day

Our family with all five grandkids

Me at Mago Retreat Center

Randy and I at Des Plaines home center

Randy and I at the Norridge Center

Our New Home

♥

O ur home center was successful for three and a half years, despite everyone's fears. We were ready for the next step.

One Sunday afternoon we drove by a for rent sign at a place in Norridge. It was just outside the city of Chicago, close to highways and twenty minutes from home. We peeked in the window, and it was full of old furniture and boxes. It was also double the size of what we needed. The space would be a great location, but we would need to start from scratch to create the space that we needed. This space had been used for family storage after relatives had passed.

The bathroom was empty, there was just a hole in the floor where the toilet was and a small glass block window with a vent. The place must have been used for storage for a long time. It was full of dirt and dust, along with a lot of old furniture.

We brought our regional manager to check out this location to give us some advice. This was the third place we brought her to, wanting her opinion since the previous two fell through.

Would this place be appropriate? Would we be able to afford a total build out? How much would it cost? Could we handle the pressure and stress of all of it? Now we would be responsible for rent and utilities. All the same questions came to our minds, just like when we started our home center. Would people come? Could we pay our bills? Could our relationship survive all the stress and the ebbs and flows of a bigger business?

We couldn't turn back at this point, feeling ready to grow from our basement center. The total build out would cost more than we had, so we asked a close relative for a contribution. We knew she had the means to back us up, and she agreed to help us out. We were beyond grateful for her generosity. Without question, the money was transferred to our account. We dug in, once again trusting the universe that it would all work out. We found a contractor, chose materials, applied for permits, and waited and waited to begin the construction.

After another eternity, the construction began, and we waited some more until we could open our doors for business. We advertised about our expected grand opening date on social media, passed out hundreds of brochures all around the area, attended benefits for seniors in the area while still maintaining classes in our home. Income was the most challenging part of having our own business, as we found out through our prior journey. The home center income was slowing down with so much focus on the Norridge center. It was a delicate balance before we could open our new center.

Another part of this was the need to share our upcoming change with our members in our home center. We had grown relationships with many people coming into our home for the past three years. We knew this move would disappoint some of them, and we knew we would lose some of them due to the distance. We hoped some of them would continue and make the drive, but we didn't know what the outcome would be. This was part of the growth of our center and changing to a new location.

We always loved what we were doing, helping others and ourselves with daily training and connecting, but we also needed to pay our bills and recurring expenses. We had to expand to move forward.

October 23, 2019, was our grand opening. People filled the training room and lobby at our new center. Many people signed up for memberships, and after three months, we had 100 members enrolled. Most of the members who took a class at the karate studio for the past three years became members at our new Norridge Center. For many of our Des Plaines Center members, Norridge was a bit farther away, so many transferred to the Mount Prospect Center. It was upsetting to lose members we had grown connected to over the years. We knew it was for the best, and we were happy they could continue their journey at another location. Mt. Prospect, after all, was where we began.

Norridge grew quickly; classes were full, and members began choosing regional workshops when they were ready. We were thrilled with our storefront studio and the location in Norridge.

We Have to Do What?

♥

In March 2020, a serious virus was spreading throughout the world. As time went by, COVID-19 hit closer to home and our studio. We thought it would go away on its own quickly, but things became more and more serious. Early April, we were forced by the government to shut down our business. People had to stay away from each other to stop the spread of this virus. Only necessary businesses could stay open with certain safety precautions. This situation created a lot of uncertainty and fear for everyone.

We had opened less than a year and were thriving, but we had no choice but to close the doors to our members. Outreaches at senior homes and assisted livings centers came to a halt since they were closed to the public. Personal coaching sessions and group classes in the studio had to stop.

We couldn't believe this was happening. We worked so hard, and our studio was booming with new members and full classes. The shutdown came up within a couple of days of being announced. We had to cancel appointments and notify members of our closing.

How could we survive like this? What could we do to keep our business and members that depended on us? We needed to help them manage stress and gain physical strength through our classes. How could we continue to pay our bills for the construction of our center and monthly expenses?

Then Came Zoom

B ody & Brain Headquarters was always supporting us. We learned about an option to continue classes and coaching sessions online. There would be some preparation to set it up, but it was a way to keep our classes going. Our basement was still set up as the Des Plaines Center. We could use the training area for our background for the online classes. We needed to figure out how to get online and get a decent camera and microphone. We had done a class online when Chicago was in a deep freeze a couple of winters before. It worked for us once or twice before, but now classes would be online every day.

We signed up for a business account on Zoom so we could host classes for more than 45 minutes, which was the free option time limit. We ordered the camera and microphone from Amazon that were recommended to us. Amazon would become the best place to shop over the next couple of years with home delivery so easy.

We began classes online within a few days of the government requiring us to close the center. We lost about 40% of our members over the next month since they didn't want to join the class online. Other members gratefully continued with the new mode of classes. I was happy to be teaching classes, which helped me to manage the stress of what was going on in the outside world as well as the members.

It was a scary time for everyone, hearing all the news of this awful virus spreading quickly and killing the elderly. Also, reports said some young people with no prior illness got seriously ill and died as well.

The isolation from others was another challenge for many people. We came up with discounts for members who continued online classes to renew early so we could pay our bills. Our landlord helped us by reducing the rent temporarily. This helped us greatly at this difficult time in our new business.

Randy & I struggled in our partnership and relationship at this time with so much uncertainty. We argued more and blamed each other because of so much stress.

I was forced to learn more about social media advertising because it was the only way to get the word out now. We previously passed out brochures door to door and left them at local stores, but everything was closed except essential businesses. We also encouraged members to refer friends and family since it was so challenging to get new people at the time. By the grace of God and the Universe, we were able to stay afloat. Luckily, we were able to get a Small Business Disaster Loan to help pay some of our expenses since we weren't making the income like before.

The world slowly opened back up again, phase by phase. We just kept doing what we could, reaching out to help others and taking good care of our members online.

Warm weather and the month of May rolled into Chicago. The COVID-19 safety rules eased up, so we could gather outside in the parks in small groups. This brought a lot of hope for us and many members who didn't join classes online. We planned a class at the park and no-tified our previous and current members about this class. Many people came to join us in the park, renewing their memberships. We were so grateful to see everyone again.

We had begun to emerge from our in-home cocoons and from all the fear that surrounded Covid. Having class in the park was healing for everyone. We all relished the freedom of being out of the house and in nature with the trees, grass, and blue skies.

Eventually we were able to start limited classes in the studio, six feet apart, of course. We could also resume our private sessions for in-per-son coaching. Little by little, we began to get back to the studio. We were happy to be back to our beautiful space we created to be with in-person classes. We also set up a camera in the ceiling of the classroom so people who weren't comfortable or too far away could continue on Zoom.

Again?

I n November, they ordered us to close again because the virus was spreading, and hospitals were overloaded. Many lives were being lost tragically at that time. Some of our members had come down with the virus along with families and friends, but nobody who was closest to us at this time.

Teresa conceived her third child during the lockdown. We were concerned about her and her future baby's well-being and our four young grandsons. We limited our visits with her and her family to outdoors when possible, visiting each of our kids separately. Thanksgiving was around the corner, but we knew we couldn't get together with our family for the holiday, to keep her and the unborn baby safe.

We would have to teach all classes online again and could do that from anywhere there was internet.

Within a week, we drove to Florida to visit Aunt Terry, who was 92 years old. She owns two duplexes, and we could stay in one next to her. While teaching classes online from there and meeting our private session members online, we could also visit her. She had been quarantined from any visiting family and friends for months. Several trips were cancelled by us and other family members that would go see her regularly before.

This road trip helped Randy and me to reconnect after the stress and tension between us because of the uncertainty of Covid and our business. Running a business together has many challenges, and with Covid, they were magnified. We had a lot of time in the car to unwind.

We talked things out about how we felt, and played fun music, dancing in our seats and singing. It was great getting away from the confines of our worries. We made resolutions to be kinder and more understanding with each other during this difficult time. Riding bikes to the beach every day and eating together on the screen porch were part of our leisurely routine between classes and online sessions. Our love and respect for each other in marriage and business were renewed.

Aunt Terry was thrilled to have the company, and we had Thanksgiving Dinner together. It was a win–win in many ways.

Back in Chicago, winter came quickly.

The holidays were quiet since we had to be cautious with the upcoming arrival of our new grandchild.

Haley Rose

♥

When I gazed into her newborn eyes, I felt my soul.

On January 23, 2021, Haley Rose was born a beautiful healthy girl, our fifth grandchild but first granddaughter!

Tears of gratitude and joy rolled down my cheeks as I gazed into her newborn eyes, feeling my soul and hers as one. She was an angel straight from heaven bringing blessings to our family once again.

Each of our five grandchildren are blessings bringing hope to our family and vision of creating a better world.

All because two people fell in love.

Happy New Year!

♥

January 2021, the first vaccine was approved for urgent use. Things started to look up with the Covid situation, thankfully so we could go back to the studio for in person classes again.

Classes were small at first. We had star stickers on the floor in the training room, marking the required 6-foot social distance. Some members wore masks, but most were okay without them in the training room. We urged them to wear masks coming in and they could be removed once they were on their star ready for class. A camera was installed in the ceiling, so while we taught people in the studio, members could also participate online.

"It's so great to see everyone in person! I missed seeing all your smiling faces in person. Now you can help me count too! Bangapsamnida, everyone!" It felt so good to be able to teach class in person. I missed going to our beautiful space and getting out of the house.

In May of 2021 I received the Covid vaccine which was the first vaccine I ever had in my life since I was excused from them being Christian Science as a kid. Randy had travelled to Sedona for a training, and I decided it was time to get the vaccine since it was available. I feared he may come home with Covid after travelling so I went to get one before he came back. I was tired for a day but glad I did it since I was around people a lot and now had a newborn grandchild.

In November 2021 we had been fully vaccinated, and our outreaches were on the schedule again and the phone was ringing. Classes were growing and we had an opportunity to have an additional teacher for the later classes to keep the number of people down per class.

Bringing Members to Sedona

♥

J ournal Entry:

I'm writing this part of my story on the airplane on my way to Sedona with three of our members from Norridge. It's been quite a rollercoaster ride these last two years from when we opened in Norridge. You never know what will emerge next, but one thing I know is we can handle whatever comes our way. We've endured Covid 19 and a new business of helping others manage stress and managing our own anxieties as well. We are grateful and blessed."

We arrived at Sedona Mago Center after the bumpy ride down Bill Gray Road.

"It's so beautiful here. The air smells so fresh, and the sound of silence is in the air," said one of my members.

"Is that rosemary? Look at the red rocks all around; it's so amazing here. I feel peace already," Another member said.

"Let's check in and rest for a while, and I'll show you my favorite place, the Healing Garden," I said.

"Okay, see you in 30 minutes," they answered.

"When we go to the healing garden, please try to be silent, listen to the sounds of nature, and be present. This is my favorite place to go to be with myself and connect to nature. I hope each of you can come here by yourself at some point this weekend."

"You can take your shoes off here if you want and walk barefoot to absorb the healing energy from the earth."

The welcome energy of peace in nature filled our bodies and minds after the long day of travel. Everyone was silent, absorbing the warm sun on our skin, the fresh air whispering through the trees, the sounds of the water, and the birds and insects singing to us. The beauty of the trees and plants with blue skies and red rock mountains in the distance took us back to our true nature.

The senior trainers and trainings are always amazing at Sedona Mago Retreat, and everyone shifted from stressed to relaxed quickly after the first session of exercise and lecture.

The meals are always another highlight of my time spent there. Fresh, healthy food prepared with love, while gathering with other members sharing our experiences is wonderful. Outside dining is always my favorite.

Two of the members that went with me made plans to go back in October 2022. Once you go, you never forget how you feel in this healing place.

Sedona Mago Center is a special place for me. The cover of this book is the Healing Garden at Sedona Mago Center.

From Mentee to Mentor

♥

You must want to fly so much that you are willing to give up being a caterpillar.

I am grateful for every member that has come and stayed and gone from our centers. Some are still with us from our home center in Des Plaines. It's always interesting to remember how magical some meetings were.

One rainy night in fall 2018, there was a networking event with the Des Plaines Chamber of Commerce. The place was in an office complex not far from the house, but the GPS instructions weren't clear. While holding my painful neck as I drove in circles and convincing myself to keep searching, I found it.

Walking in, trying to compose myself, to no avail, head in hand, breathing deeply, I scoped out the room. There were small groups of people scattered around the large office, making small talk with snacks and drinks in hand.

I checked in, got my name tag, found the restroom, and got something to eat and drink. This was never easy, head in hand, but it's how I lived. I found a group of women that I could join that seemed friendly.

"Hi, I'm JoAnn Dickson from Body & Brain Yoga Tai Chi in Des Plaines. Does anyone have any stress?"

"Ha ha! I have plenty. We are from Diamond Company; I'm Natasha and this is Sue and Diane. Where are you located?"

"My husband and I run a center in our home near Golf & Elmhurst Roads. In Des Plaines."

"Okay, great. Let's exchange cards and maybe we can work together somehow. I've been wanting to try yoga for a while," Natasha expressed. She had a genuine smile that eased my nerves and warmed my heart.

"Here's a brochure. Let me know when you want to try a class."

I followed up with Natasha shortly after our meeting, and she was busy with work and family but would reach out soon when she had time.

A couple of months later, Giacomos in Des Plaines was hosting the Christmas Lunch for the Chamber, and I donated one of Ilchi Lee's books and a free introductory session.

I saw Natasha at another table and waved hello and sat down where there was an opening with other women.

"The winner of Ilchi Lee's book and the Introductory Session from Body & Brain Yoga Tai Chi in Des Plaines is Natasha from Diamond Company."

"Natasha stood up to receive her prizes as I walked over. I guess it's a sign you need to make that appointment?"

"Oh, my gosh! I guess so. It's good to see you again."

"Yes, it's good to see you. Let's make the appointment," I encouraged.

"Ok, let me check my calendar. It will probably have to be after the holidays. I'm busy with work and my family."

We set the date for mid–January. I texted to confirm, and she said she had a migraine for three days. We rescheduled for the next week. She would have to leave work early, but she would try.

The text came. "I'm so sorry. I have to stay longer. Would it be okay if I came in an hour?"

"Okay, see you then."

As she came down the stairs, she was apologizing in a small voice, "I'm so sorry. I feel so bad. Thank you for waiting for me."

We talked openly about what was going on in her life and how it was affecting her. Next, we tapped our bodies to awaken the energy flow and focus, stretched to open our joints, followed by relaxation and breathing. As she sat up, a gentle smile appeared on her face, eyes sparkling with peace and calm. "I'm so glad I finally made it."

"Me too. I want to help you, but you have to choose yourself now," I said in a concerned voice.

"I know. I'm getting sick more now and have so much stress. I need to take care of myself."

"I recommend 10 coaching sessions. We will discuss *I've Decided to Live 120 Years* by Ilchi Lees. That's the book you won at the Christmas lunch. We'll discuss one chapter a week, and I will ask questions relating to the book and your life, and then we will exercise together. I know you are very busy, but you have to commit to this time to take care of yourself. If you skipped doing simple things like taking a shower each day or brushing your teeth because you're busy, all kinds of other problems would appear. This is necessary for your self-care."

"Okay, I agree. I'm ready."

Many appointments were canceled and postponed because of her busy schedule. I recommended workshops for her to go for and time was always an issue. After lots of guidance, love, and patience, she grew stronger in confidence and self-value.

Since 2018, Natasha has been to Finding True Self, other regional workshops, and Brain Management Training, at Sedona Mago Center for Well-Being and Retreat. She is scheduled to go back there soon. She still struggles with taking time for herself, but she does it because she knows how valuable she is.

Natasha now shares Body & Brain principles with people in her life. I'm so glad I didn't give up and go home that dark, rainy night.

Coaching her and many other members has been so precious to me. I love connecting to the members on a personal level and setting up a program to help them to improve their life. When I see how much they change and feel good about themselves after our sessions, it brings me joy.

These private sessions come naturally to me. After listening to what is going on in people's lives and what they want to work on, my intuition takes over. Words flow from my heart to theirs, along with sharing the exercises and affirmations needed to have them experience peace and hope. I have used many of Ilchi Lee's books to create coaching programs according to what the members need. I ask them to read a chapter each week and we discuss how the principles in the book relate to their life and ask questions accordingly.

I've used *I've Decided to Live 120 Years* for people who are looking for a purpose in their lives, *Connect* to help people reconnect to themselves, and *Solar Body* and *Water Up Fire Down* for basic energy principles for general health and well-being. Recently I'm utilizing the *Living Tao Timeless Principles for Everyday Enlightenment* book which teaches a path to universal principles.

Many people have benefited from these Coaching Programs by gaining personal freedom of choice, finding inner strength, improving communication skills in relationships, and increasing overall well-being in their lives.

I am grateful to have these tools available to use and the ability to share the wisdom that comes from within to help others.

Sung Cho, Butterfly of Hope

♥

When the world says give up, Hope whispers, "Try one more time."

For my 60th birthday, I took a special training at Sedona Mago Center to receive my spiritual name. For a whole week, I could focus on myself to reconnect to my purpose and vision. Through lecture and daily exercise, I connected to my dream and purpose on a deeper level. Starlight and sunrise meditation were special parts of the training that I will always remember.

While wandering around the beautiful healing garden at break time, I saw monarchs. They were orange and yellow butterflies flying freely around the colorful flowers. The butterflies reminded me of the freedom of my true self. I wanted to be free like a butterfly and embody hope for humanity.

Hope was also my mom's middle name: Shirley Hope Mayer-Santore.

Through the training, I received my spiritual name
Sung Cho, Butterfly of Hope.
Journal Entry 7/28/22:

I can't believe I've written the book I've dreamed about for several years. I'm amazed by how it has all come together. Feeling nervous about exposing some of my past and putting it out there. I don't want to hurt Randy either since he's such a big part of it. He's been so supportive by listening to me talk about my progress and challenges. He's such a good man. I love him dearly and am so grateful to have him by my side.

I want to share my experiences and how much I've changed to let others know they can change, too. I've been through a lot in my life and grown and changed in many ways through all the challenges I faced. I love helping people feel better about themselves and to find their inner strength and connection. I'm so grateful to have tools I've learned with Body & Brain to guide others.

When I am coaching or teaching class, and the words flow from my mouth without filtering from my brain I'm amazed. Life Particles come through me as words and love flowing straight to the members. It's magic. Thank you, Ilchi Lee, for your devotion and dedication to guide many people including myself and your help in my physical and emotional self-healing.

I am Butterfly of Hope, and I have Found My Wings.

Acknowledgements:

♥

I want to thank Randy my husband who stayed by my side throughout my growth process and healing and spiritual journey

He was there to listen to my fears and worries and watched me change not knowing what the results might include. We raised a family together and now we run a business together with many opportunities for growth. We encourage each other, sometimes blame each other but always support each other. He is my true soul mate, and we share the same purpose for our life.

Thanks also for reading my story and helping me with edits and ideas.

I started the writing process many times over the last several years, but last fall was the true beginning of my memoir. Nancy Stewart who is a member in Norridge, short story author and writing coach, created a mini event teaching us how to outline a memoir. During that mini event I made an outline and started filling in the chapters after. She gave me suggestions and tips introducing me to showing instead of telling my story. This was the spark of my memoir journey. Running our business takes a lot of focus so it got put on the back burner for a while. Thank you, Nancy, for all your help & encouragement!

Spring of 2022 I was searching on Facebook for writing groups which someone suggested to me. I found a 10-week course led by Carolyn V. Hamilton and through that program I finished my rough draft. I learned a lot through her program about writing and what to do and not to do through the process.

Thank you, Carolyn!

Next, I searched for someone to help me through the next step to keep going. Sue Fitzmaurice had an online program and her program taught me more of the basics. Most importantly being in her group coaching zoom calls gave me the courage to keep going. I shared my first chapter that was edited with them on one of our meetings. They were impressed by my writing and skill and gave me the courage to keep going. Thank you, Sue!

Always being on Facebook and interacting on the Writing Memoir groups, I found Maria Secoy from All Write Well. She was starting a program including coaching calls to go all the way to publishing.

Some of her Facebook Live videos impressed me, and I loved her enthusiasm. I was hesitant at first then decided it was a great opportunity since I had done my first draft and was ready for the next step.

I am currently getting ready for publishing and Maria has guided me the whole way. She and her All Write Well team have inspired and encouraged me through the self-doubt of writing my first book. I'm grateful for their help through the process.

Thanks also to Fiverr. I had three women beta-readers from this handy website. Jen, Catherine & Shelley helped me shape my story and improve it in ways that were much needed.

Also, thank you to my family for your encouragement and interest in my writing journey. Alex, Teresa, Ashley, and Nick thanks for listening with excitement and sharing ideas and possibilities with me.

A special thanks to Teresa who read my story and gave me valuable feedback, although it wasn't easy, I appreciate your honesty.

Thanks to my regional manager Magdalena Szara and our team of Illinois West, Jihee, and Julia and Leeta to name a few who have been by my side through the past several years inspiring me to stay strong.

Thank you to Oceana who has encouraged my healing and strength, connecting me to Ilchi Lee also for my healing.

Thank you to Soobok, Jung Shim and Keum Dao who have supported me with training and consultations.

Thank you to David Driscoll for helping me to clearly express my feelings and experiences with Body & Brain.

Thank you to Han Myung who shared the beautiful picture of Mago Garden for my cover at Sedona Mago Center for Well-being and Retreat and your encouragement during the training to receive my spiritual name.

Also thank you to Seong JahBi and Ilchibuko Todd for the beautiful training and love you gave during the training to receive my spiritual name Sung Cho "Butterfly of Hope"

Thank you to my teacher Ilchi Lee for creating Body & Brain, the Holistic Wellness Program that has given me my life and purpose and for sharing the BHP self-healing that gave me my strength back. I am forever grateful to you.

Self-Healing Resources:

♥

Sedona Mago Center for Well-Being and Retreat,
  sedonamagoretreat.org
  Body & Brain Yoga and Tai Chi, BodynBrain.com or youtube.com
/BodynBrain
  Finding True Self Workshop,sites.google.com/bodynbrain.com/
workshops/
  beginner/finding-true-self
  Brain Education, youtube.com/braineducationtv
  Ilchi Lee, ilchi.com or youtube.com/ilchilee

About the Author:

JoAnn Santore Dickson has been journaling her innermost thoughts and feelings since childhood.

She was raised Christian Science by her parents Shirley and Joe Santore. Youngest of four siblings David, Rick, April. They were raised in Niles, Illinois.

Randy is her husband of 40 years. She is a mother of three adult children Alex, Nicholas & Teresa. Ashley, Jon and Kateryna are part of her cherished extended family. She has been blessed with five grand-children as of today: Jase, Trevor, Owen, Travis, and Haley.

After several years of taking yoga classes through a continued educa-tion program she found Body & Brain. Having many health struggles at the time from stress she dove into the practice. Classes became a respite for her to release the stress she carried in her body.

Finding True Self Workshop in October 2014 changed her life and view of herself. She woke up to her value and realized the inner strength she had all along. She always talked about wanting to write about her experiences with Body & Brain to share how much her life changed. Now she has accomplished her dream.

JoAnn has completed the Sedona Health Coaching program, trained as a Body & Brain Franchise representative and owner and also Certi-fied as a Yoga Therapist.

She and Randy have shared Body & Brain principles since 2016, running a center in their home for 3 ½ years and now have a storefront location in Norridge, Illinois which they will celebrate 3 years in October 2022.

She loves helping people change their lives through Personal Coaching & Group Classes based on Body & Brain's Holistic Wellness Program and Ilchi Lee's books.

Her lifestyle of helping others through daily practice she acknowledges is the best opportunity to help herself also spiritually and physically.

Connect with Me:

Email <u>Norridge@BodynBrain.com</u>
Phone 708-716-3106
@BodynBrainnorridge Facebook and Instagram
Website BodynBrain.com/Norridge

Made in the USA
Monee, IL
25 October 2022

16553991R00146